"At its core, this book allows the modern to explore the deep meaning of an ageless, universal truth: Earth is a place where souls are sent to evolve. *Why?* goes beyond philosophy and offers practical guidelines for mindfully participating in one's own evolutionary process."

> —**Michael A. Singer**, author of the *New York Times* bestseller, *The Untethered Soul*

"If you have ever wondered why you're here and what your purpose is, this clear, short book, written by three wise and compassionate beings, will not only help you get your answers, but, more importantly, let you understand more deeply how to live a life attuned with your destiny."

> —**James Fadiman, PhD**, cofounder of Sofia University; author of *Psychedelic Explorer's Guide: Safe, Therapeutic, and Sacred Journeys*

"Happiness happens when we remove the blinders and obstacles, so we can see what was there all along. This very wise book is a gem. If you are seeking greater fulfillment and joy in your life, please avail yourself of this splendid, simple, and practical guide."

> —**Larry Dossey, MD**, author of *The Power of Premonitions* and *Reinventing Medicine*

"In this book, timeless questions surrounding life purpose and calling are addressed in accessible, inspirational, and practical ways. A relevant book for anyone, at any age, in any culture!"

—**Angeles Arrien, PhD**, cultural anthropologist, author of *The Four-Fold Way* and *Living in Gratitude*

"This little book has a very big goal, nothing less than helping readers discover their life purpose. They accomplish this task by pulling from the wisdom of the past, as well as by providing provocative exercises that direct readers toward self-knowledge. Many books have similar goals, but few have succeeded as well as McKay, ÓLaoire, and Metzner, and have done so in such an engaging and reader-friendly style."

—**Stanley Krippner**, PhD, coauthor of *Personal Mythology* and *Demystifying Shamans and Their World*

WHY?

What Your Life Is Telling You
about Who You Are and Why You're Here

MATTHEW McKAY, PhD
SEÁN ÓLAOIRE, PhD
RALPH METZNER, PhD

New Harbinger Publications, Inc.

Publisher's Note

This publication is designed to provide accurate and authoritative information in regard to the subject matter covered. It is sold with the understanding that the publisher is not engaged in rendering psychological, financial, legal, or other professional services. If expert assistance or counseling is needed, the services of a competent professional should be sought.

Distributed in Canada by Raincoast Books

Copyright © 2013 by Matthew McKay, Seán ÓLaoire, and Ralph Metzner
New Harbinger Publications, Inc.
5674 Shattuck Avenue
Oakland, CA 94609
www.newharbinger.com

Cover design by Amy Shoup; Text design by Michele Waters-Kermes; Acquired by Catharine Meyers; Edited by Nelda Street

Library of Congress Cataloging-in-Publication Data

McKay, Matthew.
  Why? : what your life is telling you about who you are and why you're here / Matthew McKay, PhD, Se?n ?Laoire, PhD, and Ralph Metzner, PhD.
    pages cm
  ISBN 978-1-60882-775-6 (pbk. : alk. paper) -- ISBN 978-1-60882-776-3 (pdf e-book) -- ISBN 978-1-60882-777-0 (epub) 1. Self-perception. 2. Self-realization. 3. Conduct of life. I. ?Laoire, Se?n. II. Metzner, Ralph. III. Title.
  BF697.5.S43M35 2013
  170'.44--dc23

                          2012047473

Printed in the United States of America

15   14   13

10   9   8   7   6   5   4   3   2   1   First printing

For Catharine Meyers, my dear soul friend who
keeps lighting the way.
—Matt

For Arlen;
m'Anamchara;
La'olam Va'ed.
—Seán

To my daughter, Sophia Marija Metzner, who is
finding her unique way among the life paths.
—Ralph

CONTENTS

PREFACE

The old saying "Everywhere you go, there you are" is the experience at the core of this book. Everywhere you go, there is your pain, there is your hope, there is your loss, there is what you care about. You carry it all with you; there is no escape. Try as you might to get away from pain, to fill your life with pleasure and good things, pain keeps showing up.

There is something else you can't escape: the reason why you are here. You have a purpose for being on this planet, and you can find and embrace that purpose or hide from it. Everywhere you go, that purpose will be there. Every day of your life will bring a chance to make that choice again.

When you hide from your purpose, your reason for being here, life bears the unmistakable mark of that avoidance: sadness, emptiness, and shame. When you seek your purpose—no matter what kinds of pain you also bear—your life has vitality and direction, and you feel that it is *about* something.

This book is in your hands to answer one question: Why? Why are you here? Why are you living this life? To do that, we'll have to examine what life—consciousness—really is and what all the other conscious beings are doing on this planet.

The answer is personal and unique to you. No other soul has exactly the same purpose. Knowing your purpose is like knowing the deepest secret about yourself, one that will release you from the trap of pleasure and pain, one that will shine a bright light on the path ahead, one that can show you true happiness.

Part 1

WHAT WE KNOW

1

THE PURSUIT OF
HAPPINESS

You have been on this planet for some time, and you know one thing very well: it's hard. In crucial ways, life is different than you would have hoped it would be. Some of the things you sought or dreamed of never happened. Some of the people you loved or counted on the most are gone. And sometimes, in the midst of busy streets and headlong days, you feel solitary. You feel invisible, as if your struggles and fears were yours alone. And even in the rooms called home, you sense a distance between you and others. Caught in their concerns, they live a life you cannot fully know. And you do the same.

The problem is this: On planet Earth, your pain *is* your own. Loss, failure, illness, and especially your own death are private experiences. No one can fully share them with you. On some level, much of what we do is an attempt to cope with this. We're constantly in motion, building emotional, career, and domestic castles to protect ourselves from the massive, uncontrollable forces that surround our lives. We try to connect deeply, intimately. We try to be successful, perhaps even recognized for our accomplishments. And we try to create a home that's a haven from all that might threaten us.

In the end, despite all of our planning and constant effort, we can't save ourselves from where we live: this planet and our own fragile bodies. We still face pain— emotional or physical—every day. And everyone around us, no matter how big their houses or cars or jobs, is in exactly the same place.

Cultural Hypnosis

Every culture in every part of the world attempts to answer this question: how best can we deal with our fate? In spite of all of our vulnerabilities and pain, how do we steer our lives toward some purpose? Western cultures generally support the right and need of every individual to pursue happiness. Jeremy Bentham, the philosopher who developed utilitarianism, argued that all political decisions should be based on the "greatest good for the greatest number." And the idea that government should support our pursuit of happiness is written into the US Declaration of Independence.

As psychological science developed, Sigmund Freud and the psychoanalysts, and B. F. Skinner and the behaviorists, shaped a cultural belief that the main function of a human being is to seek pleasure and avoid pain. Our lives were conceived as a long series of choices to enhance happiness and minimize unnecessary suffering.

Madison Avenue—through constant hypnotic messages in the media—tells us exactly how to do this. We should consume as much as we can afford and then borrow to consume more. The media also tell us that we should have prestigious, powerful, and lucrative employment. Without that, the message goes, we'll be reduced to a life of yearning and disappointment. Happiness requires that life be peppered with vacations, toys, and pleasurable events—and that we have machines to do our work. All of this takes money, of course, which becomes a measure of worth.

Perhaps the most important thing of all that we could have or pursue is sex. The media insist on this.

Love and belonging are the prize, but sex is the portal, the way to get there. We are taught to see ourselves as failures if we don't have an attractive partner or the ability to find willing bedmates. By linking happiness to sex and romantic love, the cultural message is that we'll be locked out of real life satisfaction without this type of intimacy.

The relentless pursuit of happiness is only part of our cultural coaching. The other message is that we must avoid pain. Pain is seen as unnecessary or embarrassing, a product of bad choices or personal failure. When pain comes, we're encouraged to use analgesics. Take a pill; take a drink. Numb out with TV or the Internet. Buy something. But whatever we do, pain is a sign of failure, and we must stop it.

These cultural injunctions about pain are why it's so difficult to be sick, old, or sad. As we face necessary losses and grieve over the ways our lives have changed, we are told on some level that we no longer fit, that we should disappear so as not to embarrass ourselves or disturb others.

The Pursuit of Happiness Doesn't Work

Chasing happiness doesn't help us find it. You already suspect this. You've been busy coping with difficult challenges and seeking a good life, a happy life. Yet you are often tired, at times sad. No matter what you do, pain continues to show up, and happiness seems momentary, ephemeral. To see why, it might be useful to differentiate among happiness, joy, and pleasure.

Let's start with joy. Joy is not happiness. Rather, it is the beauty of the moment, fully experiencing what's happening right now. That's why people enjoy sports, hobbies, traveling, kissing, creating, walking in the woods, watching a sunset, and so on. All of these experiences keep us in the now, focused on our senses, fully engaged in the present. We aren't thinking about bad things that happened in the past or dangers lurking in the future. We aren't sad or anxious; we're just here, feeling and fully living this moment in time.

You can tell why joy doesn't last. Sooner or later we leave the moment. We put down our quilting or our paintbrushes. The tennis game or the kiss ends. The sunset fades; the air gets cold and we go inside. But here's the paradox: joy doesn't end because those moments end. Joy ends because we leave the moment. The trip or tennis game or mountain hike is merely a vehicle to keep us in the now. While our attention might simply move on to the next moment, it usually doesn't. Instead, our minds slip to the future or the past, pulling up worries or judgments about ourselves or others. Joy doesn't last, because without some focusing activity, we leave the moment. And only in the moment is joy possible.

Pleasure, too, is often confused with happiness. There are pleasure centers in the brain that get stimulated by the release of key neurotransmitters (endorphins). Subjectively, this often feels like excitement. While we sometimes call this feeling "happiness," it is not an emotion. It's a neurological experience that *cannot last*. The reason is this: No matter how intensely pleasurable something is, the body and nervous system habituate to it. We get used to the stimulation, and our excitement eventually drops to baseline—*even if the pleasurable stimulation continues at a high level.*

All mammals desensitize to stimuli. This process of getting used to everything—pain as well as pleasure—helps us survive. Sooner or later the nervous system calms down, no matter how impactful the experience might be. Joy and pleasure fade, regardless of what we do. While they are likely to return, *we cannot keep these experiences.*

Now, finally, let's look at happiness. The emotion of happiness isn't a peak experience like joy or pleasure. When people describe the experience of happiness, they often use the word "contentment": a feeling that things are as they should be, that our lives are right and we are somehow living in a way that makes sense. But what is contentment—happiness—about, and how do we create it?

There are two kinds of contentment: happiness with what happens, the events of your life; and happiness with how you've chosen to live, the things you *do* in your life. We have little control over the contentment derived from events. Our children will or won't graduate from college, we will or won't get seriously ill, our mortgages are or aren't underwater, and we have or haven't suffered a family loss. But what we can control, and the happiness that's within our reach, derives from the ways we choose to live.

Happiness comes and can be sustained by making choices that are aligned with the ideals that matter most to us: our life purpose. This kind of happiness is *not* ephemeral. It can't be taken away. No misfortune or illness can strip it from us. No rejection, no job loss, no market plunge can touch it. This happiness rests on the knowledge that regardless of the outcome, we have done what mattered. We have acted on our highest values.

Achieving the happiness of a life based on the deep truth of *how* we want to be—not what we want to happen—is what this book is about.

Staying Happy

Happiness is your birthright; it is the natural state of the soul. This deep, core serenity can remain undisturbed by the trials and setbacks of living. In fact this serenity, this sense of groundedness and contentment, can actually grow from hardships and the ways in which we face them. It can grow from pain. The trick is to learn how to mine all experiences, pleasurable or painful, and find their embedded gold. Every experience presents an opportunity to act from your core purpose. So it is not where you look that brings happiness, but how you look. If you don't know how to look for these opportunities, you can search everywhere and find nothing. When you do learn how to look, you can search everywhere and find everything.

While there is a direct, positive correlation between happiness and alignment with your life purpose, there is a direct, negative correlation between happiness and the pleasure-pain agenda. We can spend our time searching for ways of protecting and pleasuring ourselves, yet find security and serenity evasive. When we are seduced by society's clarion calls offering pain relief or consumer pleasures, we become obsessed with having something that doesn't exist: a life where pleasure is constant and pain can always be kept at bay. This is the road to suffering.

Staying happy requires abandoning the pleasure-pain agenda and seeking—in every situation—the chance to do what aligns with your deepest values. This book will show you how.

2

WHY ARE WE HERE?

Those busy, sad, and lonely days show up in our lives for a reason. The sense of being disconnected, perhaps even invisible, and that feeling of being busy, yet passionless and uninspired, exist for a reason. The impression that something is missing, that there is some lack of purpose or direction, wells up again and again, like a demand for attention by some ignored child. These experiences all come from the same fountainhead. They are a special kind of pain whose source is amnesia, a forgetting of why we're here.

When you forget the reason why you're here, every life choice is a blind one. You find yourself choosing friends and partners and jobs and communities without a sense of where you're headed or what truly matters. Life becomes a collection of events, obligations, disappointments, and moments of relief—a long effort to avoid pain and find pleasure. And happiness becomes a visitor, showing up at odd moments and disappearing again. The more we seek it, the more it seems to recede.

Why does our purpose here remain such a mystery when all around us are people who are offering their answers? From the pulpits and religious broadcasts, we are given one model: we have come here to be tested and earn salvation. Madison Avenue gives us a different view: we are here to consume, find pleasure, and live a long, happy life. The media message is a variant of Madison Avenue. Movies, TV, and magazines create the impression that life is about finding a beautiful sexual partner, acquiring money and status, and scheduling a steady stream of exciting activities. Some spiritual traditions suggest yet another life purpose: taking care of others. One's work in life is, therefore, to support family, community, sentient beings, and the world itself. You probably know people who have woven a life purpose out of one or more of these messages, and many of these same people are living busy, sad, and lonely days.

Learning why you're here may take setting aside some of these traditional ideas and concepts. It involves awakening what you already know about yourself but have forgotten because of the cultural hypnosis we are all prey to. The first step toward remembering why you're here is to get clearer about the nature of human consciousness.

Consciousness Survives outside the Body

Most religious and spiritual traditions teach that the soul survives the death of the body. Until very recently, however, there was no real evidence for this belief. Now, through first-person reports of *near-death experiences* (NDEs), there is clear evidence that consciousness can leave the body. Raymond Moody Jr.'s groundbreaking book *Life After Life* was the first to bring the NDE to public attention. Through interviews with many people who had clinically died and were later resuscitated, Moody established the now-familiar sequence of near-death events: consciousness leaves the body, hovers briefly overhead (often watching the medical efforts to sustain life), heads up a dark tunnel, arrives at a place of light and peace and love, is met by guides or deceased loved ones, and is finally directed to return to the body.

What Moody found, in many of these accounts, was that NDEs included the ability to see, hear, and remember experiences that the mortally ill person could never have known about. Often these were things that others did and said while the ill person was unconscious. For example, there are many reports where a near-death individual, eyes closed and under anesthetic, was later able to describe the appearance, behavior, gestures, and facial expressions of medical personnel whom the individual had never met. Furthermore, many near-death experiencers were able, despite being unconscious during a lifesaving procedure, to describe details of the room that couldn't be seen from where they lay. Some of these details included descriptions, which were later confirmed, about what was on top of a fluorescent light fixture or a high cabinet, or about hidden scars and birthmarks of medical staff. There were even detailed descriptions of unusual footwear (not visible to the patient).

Perhaps the most astonishing of these NDE accounts is provided by Kenneth Ring in the book *Lessons from the Light*. A critical-care social worker named Kimberly Clark reported interviewing a patient named Maria at Harborview Medical Center in Seattle. The patient was a migrant worker who had experienced a heart attack while visiting Seattle for the first time. She had spent two days in the hospital's coronary-care unit and then had a cardiac arrest. The day after her attack, Maria described to Clark a very detailed and extraordinary NDE. For a period of time during the resuscitation procedures, Maria had looked down on herself from the top of the room. However, she soon had found herself moving through the walls and outside the hospital. There she had risen along the north wing of the building and eventually had become interested in an object on the ledge of the third floor. It was a tennis shoe. Maria had studied the shoe, noticing that one of the laces was tucked beneath the heel and observing a small worn place on the toe.

Kimberly Clark, who was an NDE skeptic, listened to the account without much interest. Clark would likely never have bothered to check out the story if Maria hadn't begged her to find the shoe. Clark did go to the third floor of the north wing and found the shoe in the exact condition that Maria had described.

Kenneth Ring reaches this conclusion about Maria's case:

> What is the probability that a migrant worker visiting a large city for the first time, who suffers a heart attack and is rushed to a hospital at night, would, while having a cardiac arrest, simply "hallucinate" seeing a tennis shoe—with very specific and unusual features—on the ledge

of a floor higher than her physical location in the hospital?

The answer, of course, is highly unlikely—unless consciousness can leave the body, enabling one to see and hear things that otherwise couldn't be observed. If this were the only case of its kind, we might be able to dismiss it as an aberration. However, there are multiple cases in which dying patients observed what they could never have seen or known, and these observations were later verified.

As reported by Kenneth Ring, Michael Sabom, a cardiologist, was the first to do extensive research on cardiac patients who had reported having out-of-body experiences during surgery or cardiac arrests. These patients described details of the treatment protocols, the appearance of medical personnel, and the treatment environment. Sabom then tried to confirm these accounts. He interviewed members of the medical team and other witnesses and examined medical records to determine how much of what these patients saw and heard could be verified. Sabom concluded that there was overwhelming evidence that these patients were accurately reporting treatment details that they could not possibly have known.

These NDE accounts lead to the unmistakable conclusion that consciousness can leave the body and that conscious perception in no way depends on the body for the ability to see, hear, or "think." Paradoxically, NDE accounts describe a sharpening of perception once consciousness leaves the body. Some NDE reports suggest that literally hundreds of perceptions can get processed simultaneously, in a 360-degree view.

If we are not dependent on the body for perception and thought, then we are capable of a sustained existence outside of our physical shells. But this raises another important question: why would a nonphysical consciousness enter a body and reside in that body throughout all its vicissitudes until death? To answer that, we need to examine the next critical fact of human experience.

The Same Consciousness Can Reside Serially in More Than One Body

As reported in *Life Before Life*, by Dr. Jim Tucker, Dr. Ian Stevenson (who wrote the foreword for that book and also wrote *Twenty Cases Suggestive of Reincarnation* and *Children Who Remember Previous Lives*), over the course of forty years, interviewed children from all over the world who had memories of past lives. More than 2,500 of these cases are registered in the files of the Division of Perceptual Studies at the University of Virginia. These children typically begin talking about past-life experiences shortly after developing language skills, and the memories fade and disappear altogether by the age of seven or eight. Stevenson—and later, Dr. Jim Tucker, who continued his research—made every effort to solve these cases by trying to match names, events, and locations given by the child with the lives of deceased individuals. Many of the children knew the name of a previous family they claimed to be their own. Many knew the names of previous husbands, wives, and children; the location of a previous home; and detailed events of a previous life.

Of 971 cases that were studied closely, 702 were solved as follows: In 195 cases, the previous personality was part of the child's family. In another 60, the child's current family had a close association to the previous personality's family. In 115 cases, there was only a slight association between families. In 93 cases, the child's family had known of the previous personality but was in no way associated with the individual. Finally, there were 239 solved stranger cases, where the child reported a previous personality who lived in a distant city or even a different country. These 239 stranger cases are obviously the most interesting, because the child was able to give such detailed information about the previous personality that researchers, often using historical records, could find out who this person was. Several stories follow that are typical of these solved stranger cases.

A good example of a long-distance case is that of Kimal Atasoy. This six-year-old boy from Turkey reported memories of a life in Istanbul, more than five hundred miles from his current home. The boy told investigators that his previous family's name was Karakas and that he had lived in a three-story house on the water, where boats were tied up. There was a church behind the house, and his next-door neighbor was a woman named Aysegul. Kimal further reported that he had been an Armenian Christian and that his wife had been Greek Orthodox, that he had often carried a leather bag, and that he had only lived in the house part of the year.

Kimal and his mother had never been to Istanbul, and his father had only visited the city twice on business. Kimal's current family was Muslim, and they knew no Armenians. There was absolutely no possibility that Kimal could have known anything about the family in Istanbul. Nevertheless, the three-story house belonging to the Karakas family was found. It was built on the water with a church behind it. The deceased Karakas had been an Armenian Christian, and his wife had been Greek Orthodox. He had dealt in leather goods and had always carried a large leather bag. It was also confirmed that Karakas had lived in the house only during the summer months.

Another case illustrating many typical features of past-life memories is that of Nazih al-Danaf of Lebanon. As a child, he began reporting memories of a life in which he had carried pistols and lived in a two-story house surrounded by trees with a cave nearby. In this other life, he'd had a wife and young children, and a mute friend, and he had been murdered.

Nazih eventually persuaded his parents to take him to a small town ten miles away—a place he'd never visited before. There he was able to give directions to the home of his previous personality and to the nearby cave. On entering his previous residence, he was able to confirm many intimate details of his life to the widow who lived there. This included identifying the cabinet where he'd kept his guns, the name of the man who'd built a foundation for the house, the details of an accident suffered by the previous personality, the cause of a daughter's illness (she'd taken some of her father's pills), the fact that he'd given his brother a Checki 16 pistol, the name and location of his first wife, and the names of friends and a deceased brother.

It was also confirmed that the previous personality had a mute friend. And when the brother (recipient of the Checki 16 pistol) tried to trick Nazih by showing him the wrong gun, the boy said that it was not the same pistol he had given him.

One more case closer to home might be useful to review. A retired New York City policeman named John McConnel, who was working as a security guard, was shot six times during a robbery and died. Five years after McConnel had died, his daughter gave birth to a son, William. When the boy was about three, he began referring to himself as his mother's daddy. This toddler knew the name of his grandfather's long-dead cat, that he had died on a Thursday night (even though the boy didn't yet know the days of the week), and details about the grandfather's relationship to his mother. Most amazingly, he knew specifics about the shooting that even his mother had never known.

These cases, and the 702 others that were solved, provide strong evidence that consciousness can move from one body to another, that memories and identity from a previous life can be retained in a subsequent one. Why would this be? What purpose would it serve for a conscious entity to live more than one life, often in different families and different locations, and always with different circumstances and challenges? The only reasonable answer is that each life offers opportunities for new experiences—experiences that allow an individual consciousness to learn and grow. One life is not enough for the full development of a soul. And a single life is not a make-or-break test of the soul's worth. Salvation isn't the point of living—learning is.

Consciousness Exists between Lives

Many years ago, psychologist Michael Newton, a specialist in behavior therapy and hypnosis, was treating a woman who suffered from chronic loneliness. Though a skeptic about so-called past life regressions, Newton had learned to use them to explain, and often relieve, certain present life difficulties.

When the induction was complete, the client began reporting, to Newton's astonishment, detailed descriptions of a *life between lives*. These included seeing her soul group (essentially, a cohort of souls who all reincarnate and study together), whom she deeply missed. Newton identified key phrases that had induced this memory and used them with several more clients. They described being met by guides at the moment of transition, commencing a life-review process, meeting with a council of elders to examine what was learned and accomplished in the past life, rejoining a soul group, engaging in multiple lessons with guides, and eventually selecting another life to continue these lessons in a physical existence.

Newton was intrigued. He subsequently hypnotized hundreds of clients, and amazingly, they reported nearly identical experiences from a life between lives. These experiences, the same as those previously noted, were described without prompting or preparation. Newton asked what people observed and moved them sequentially through events but never suggested what they would see next. The similarity of these many accounts is striking, because they were recorded long before Newton's book *Journey of Souls* was published. These people didn't know what to expect and came to the experience fully naive about the details of a life between lives.

Memories uncovered by hypnosis are notoriously inaccurate. Often these "memories" turn out to be false or fabricated from multiple events. What makes Newton's research extraordinary is that these many life-between-life accounts are *all essentially the same*.

What can we make of this? The first obvious conclusion is that we have multiple lives; many of the people in Newton's research reported hundreds of past existences. And there is another conclusion: between lives, our focus is on learning; we are uncovering the reasons for everything that's happened in our many lives, studying each choice, and distilling the deep truth of every lesson. Our work—both in the soul groups where we grow as discarnates and in physical bodies where we face specific, planned challenges—is to gather wisdom. We are not proving ourselves worthy of some heaven; we are *improving* ourselves.

Simply stated, we are here to see, to know, to gather whatever wisdom each life offers—and to make use of that wisdom as our souls mature and grow through each incarnation.

3

CHOICES

What carves the contour of our lives, like a slowly evolving sculpture, are the choices we make. In the Christian, Muslim, and other traditions, life choices are framed as decisions between right and wrong with a goal of earning a place in heaven. But the fact that we live multiple lives suggests that our choices have a different meaning. Rather than facing a single pass-fail test, scored on the basis of religious canon, we are in school. Over many lifetimes, the school on this planet helps us learn to do one thing: make choices that are in alignment with our reasons for being here. Big or small, everything we choose brings us closer to or farther away from our life purpose.

Why We Come Here

Life on this planet is formidable. It's a place of great beauty; there are moments of unalloyed joy and passion. But it's also a place where we lose everything: many of our dreams, our loves, our health, and ultimately our lives. It is a place where every day has a measure of unavoidable pain. Why would we come to a school like this? What unique sort of education does it offer? The answer, of course, is the pain itself.

For choices to be meaningful, they must occur in an environment where there is authentic emotional or physical risk. We have to face adversity, the experience of feeling hurt. A choice has no significance if it doesn't have consequences. In this school, everything we do is met with pleasure or pain; we can't escape that. And it imbues the decisions we make with significance. The things we do matter—in their effect on us and others—and it is only in such an environment that action-based learning takes place.

Action-based learning isn't the same as acquiring a new cognitive or conceptual understanding. It isn't about learning some abstract idea. It is learning how to *be* or *become* something; it is learning to evolve through doing. No being can change—fundamentally—except through action, through choices. So that's why we're

27

here: to choose in the face of pain so that our consciousness can grow.

The Role of Amnesia

Greek mythology describes the river Lethe: the river of forgetting that souls bathe in. And the myth is true. We arrive here in a state of amnesia, having forgotten the life between lives, having forgotten our purpose in coming here.

What cruel design would bring us to such a difficult place, a planet with unimaginable forms of suffering, where we have no memory of why we came or what we hope to learn here? It seems like a setup for failure: we have a mission of great importance and a goal to learn and do specific things in a place full of danger and adversity, but we have no idea what that mission is.

Yet amnesia is critical to our success. If we knew where we came from and were certain of what we came to do, we wouldn't take this place seriously. The dramas of this life are just a play that we've agreed to act in. But if we knew that, the choices we make here wouldn't be real. We'd be speaking and moving from a script. We'd see through the crises and the plotting devices; we'd know the climax and the denouement. Because the play and its reasons would be transparent, we would learn nothing.

Consider for a moment the experience of loss. We live in constant danger of losing what we love, what we depend on, and that danger exerts a constant influence on our choices. Then, sooner or later, the worst happens. We lose a parent, a spouse, or a child. We lose a job or a house or some physical capacity. Our minds circle around this searing pain, seeking a way to survive. And in the process, we make huge choices. Will we numb or suppress the pain? Will we support others who are also suffering? Will we run away? Will we rebuild from the damage?

But what if we knew that every actor who "died" in our play could be found in the green room afterward? What if everything lost would be returned to us, and even our aging, broken bodies would someday be replaced?

If we knew all of this, nothing truly would be lost. No meaningful choices would be made with mere temporary absences. And nothing would be learned.

So amnesia is necessary—but at such a cost. Now we must navigate through the pleasure and pain of this world with no map, no clear direction. After bathing in the river Lethe, we suffer a profound silence from our own soul histories. Filling that silence is the noise of a thousand priests, pundits, and gurus telling us what to believe and do. And above that silence is the shout of our own desires, the keening of our own fears. No wonder we lose our way.

The Illusion of Separation

A second challenge we face here is that we simply don't recognize each other. In the life between lives, each soul feels joined to every other soul. There's a sense of oneness. According to Michael Newton's research, small groups of souls often reincarnate together over many lifetimes. And any two souls may experience many forms of relationship across time: sibling, parent, spouse, neighbor, friend, teacher, or pupil.

Yet we retain so little of this consciously. We have, it's true, the occasional odd sense of recognition—or ephemeral moments of great closeness. But mostly we feel alone, isolated inside our own bodies. Mostly we feel invisible—even to souls who have known us for millennia.

On this planet, we live at great emotional distances from each other. And pain makes us even more remote, imploding us, leaving us miles from the nearest house.

The illusion of separation exists for a reason. Without it our primary work would be impossible. While each of us is here to learn individual lessons, we are all here to learn how to love in the face of pain. That's the greatest lesson this planet offers.

How do we know this—that learning to love is our first and greatest task? When you ask people to examine their core values by writing an ideal epitaph—a sentence or two that describes what they hope will be their highest achievement in life—they write about whom they loved. In thousands of cases. Not their financial or career highlights. Not books they wrote or things they built. Not houses bought or amazing journeys. The epitaph is almost always whom and how they loved.

EXERCISE: Your Epitaph

If you'd like to try the epitaph exercise yourself, here's how to do it. Imagine that it is some years from now and you have died. An epitaph is about to be carved onto your gravestone. In one or two sentences, it will capture what your life has been about. Make it your ideal, your highest value, even if you have yet to fully achieve it. On a piece of paper, start with the words: "Here lies _____. S/he was _____." And then finish the epitaph as you hope it would be written. If you wish, you can write a second epitaph reflecting what could be said about your life if you died right now. Notice any divergence between the ideal and your "current" epitaph.

So this is part of our core work: while feeling separated and alone, caught and unseen inside our bodies, we seek connection, acceptance, and the beauty in each other. And this struggle to love takes place in a soup of emotional and physical pain. We get hurt, afraid, ashamed; we feel wrong and lost and angry. And through all of this, we are trying to find (and act on) that thread of love that connects us.

The Question of Free Will

Every choice brings us closer to our life purpose or further away from it. We are here to choose. Every hour; every minute. Our bodies and minds are a vessel in which decisions are formed so action can be taken. We observe what happens after each choice, and those observations become the source of our personal wisdom. A baby chooses to crawl from a high step, and falls. That outcome—the first awareness of gravity—will influence other choices. Each experience shapes everything that follows. Our aim is to pay attention to the consequences of those actions and learn from them.

Clearly, our choices are important. But at the same time, they are limited. They're not only shaped by our experience, they are constrained by circumstances. How much freedom do we really have?

Consider individuals with brain damage, severe addictions, or serious mental illness such as schizophrenia. Or consider people born with genetic flaws resulting in impulse disorders, psychopathy, or *emotion dysregulation* (the tendency to get overwhelmed by intense emotional reactions). These souls live in bodies that make freewill decisions difficult or impossible. It would hardly be fair if, in their one chance at life and salvation, they were punished for having made "bad" choices.

Even people with more typical minds struggle to make choices given the influences of pleasure and pain. In any decision, the same two opposing factors are always in play: *drive* (the motivation to do something) and *inhibition* (the pain or fear that blocks action). If drive is significantly stronger than inhibition, or vice versa, the reinforcers of pleasure and pain will mostly determine what we do. Since drive and inhibition are typically not in balance, it usually takes an act of will—sometimes a very challenging one—to make a decision that is truly our own, overcoming the influence of rewards and punishments.

EXERCISE: "What's My Choice?"

If you want to explore the issue of will in your own life, consider completing this exercise.

1. Start by writing down five significant things you did or didn't do during the past month that involved some sort of decision (where you had at least one other choice).

2. For each of these decisions, draw two circles. The first circle represents what made you want to do it (drive) and the strength of that motivation. This circle can be big or small; the stronger your drive, the larger the circle. The second circle represents what made you afraid or reluctant to do it (inhibition). Here again, the stronger the inhibition, the larger the circle. The "drive" circle and the "inhibition" circle may be the same size, or one may be much larger than the other.

3. Then, for each decision, ask yourself whether the choice you made was mostly your own. Was your decision limited by the forces of drive and inhibition, or did you feel like you were able to consciously choose?

4. If you felt you were able to choose, how difficult was it (on a scale of 1 to 10) to use your free will in this situation?

5. For each decision, how does the difficulty relate to the difference in size between the "drive" circle and the "inhibition" circle?

As you examine the results of this exercise, you may find that it clarifies the relationship between will and reinforcers in decision making. Many people discover that it's not too hard to make decisions freely when drive and inhibition are about equal. It can be much harder to use your will when drive is much stronger than inhibition, or vice versa.

So here's the core issue: Many of the challenges and struggles we face contain powerful forces that overwhelm our will. Or—as is many times the case—our ability to use our will is physiologically or psychologically damaged. We simply, at that moment, don't have much choice in the matter. Fortunately, we aren't here to be judged for our mistakes. We're here to learn from them. And we can learn regardless of the degree of will we possess. We're still making decisions, and they can still help us learn. We are experiencing many forms of joy and pain—and learning from all of them.

For example, even a life spent as a helpless addict can be full of lessons. We may be learning about the pain of addiction in order to have greater compassion in future lives, learning about choices that led to addiction, learning how to love while addicted, or learning how to seek some form of our life purpose while basic human functions, thinking, feeling, reacting, perceiving, and will are compromised.

A lifetime spent as a criminal, a self-serving politician, a homeless outcast, or a vengeance-seeking terrorist isn't a bad or failed life. It is a life where great learning can take place. And each decision—regardless of whether it was freely chosen—has consequences that we grow from.

So no life is a lost chance. Every life builds awareness and wisdom that souls carry—despite amnesia—in some residual form (often gut feelings and intuition). Every outcome observed creates wisdom, whether the choice was made freely or made unconsciously, coerced by pain and pleasure. Willpower strengthens as we learn from the consequences of our acts over many lives. So everything we do, every decision, is important, because there is always a lesson inside each choice.

Life Purpose

While our core life purpose—to love in the face of pain—is enduring, each life has a parallel, specific purpose. Our specific life purpose evolves based on:

- *Karma*, what we have or haven't done in previous lives that must be balanced in this one

- The needs of souls who are reincarnating around us

- What we need to do and learn right now to evolve as souls

Without access to past-life memories and without knowing the plans for souls around us, we aren't likely to learn much about the first and second points. But there's a real chance that you can use tools found in this book to uncover more about the last point: what you came here to learn and do.

An examination of hypnotic regressions to life between lives (conducted by Michael Newton and hypnotherapists at the Newton Institute) reveals that each lifetime involves a very specific lesson. Case 64 in Newton's book *Destiny of Souls* is an example of a life that was about learning one thing. A young man who liked high risk and fast cars, and who'd led previous lives full of hubris and disregard for the pain of others, developed ALS (amyotrophic lateral sclerosis) at age twenty-seven. He was placed on a respirator and died at age twenty-nine in significant pain.

The lesson, gleaned from information in the life between lives, was humility. The best way to learn about the feelings of those who struggle and suffer was to experience helplessness. This man had agreed to enter a body that would provide the precise experiences he would need to move beyond his many egocentric lives.

Case 65 in *Destiny of Souls* illustrates how each return to Earth also requires us to take action, to do something that challenges entrenched behavior patterns developed over previous lives. A part-time secretary, who'd completed a nursing degree but lacked the confidence to work as an RN, explored her plan for this life. Under hypnosis, this woman discovered that she'd taken refuge in strict religious communities over previous incarnations, feeling safe and comforted by ritual practices. But, despite spiritual growth, her lives had been disconnected from others. Her caring had always been expressed from a distance. In her current life was a new core task: learning to nurture and soothe—a process that would require the strength to leave what was safe and familiar for hands-on work in a hospital.

Joelle McGonagle, of the Newton Institute, reports (in *Memories of the Afterlife*, edited by Michael Newton) about a series of hypnotic sessions that exemplify how twin life purposes combine—to learn something and do something. Her client was a fortyish woman who'd lost both her brother and seventeen-year-old son to suicide. She was wrecked by the pain. When this woman entered the life between lives, it became clear that these losses had been given to her so that she could learn courage— not just endurance or the ability to take blows, but also the willingness to fully embrace life, no matter how much it hurt. Right next to this lesson was a key task: finding new ways to care for herself. Instead of self-hate over a son's death, she was learning to protect her spirit with acceptance, with the sweet memories of love that were a source of comfort.

Our Work

This, finally, is our work: to love while we feel pain, and then to learn the lesson of this life—what we came here to become and what we seek to do.

4

How Culture Shapes Life Purpose

The guidance system of our lives and our life mission can be thought of as a computer. Your computer has two main components, the hardware—which is the physical box, mouse, monitor, and so on—and the software, which is the programs that drive it, such as the operating system, search engines, and so on. So hardware is to software as the generic human is to his or her surrounding culture. The human usually comes in at birth with all of the necessary parts present and functional, and ready to develop at age-appropriate intervals. This is the hardware. And this person will manifest these generic components in an individually unique fashion. This uniqueness, as noted earlier, is an important key to figuring out your life purpose.

And each human is born into a culture that imprints language, values, and beliefs on him or her. This is the software part. Software will significantly influence a person's life choices, particularly if he or she doesn't travel to other cultures or think deeply beyond mere parochial programming.

Computer hardware has evolved very significantly over the last fifty years; today, a single modern laptop has more computing power than all of the massive mainframe computers from 1970 combined.

Similarly, human hardware has evolved from *Homo erectus* (upright-walking beings) to *Homo sapiens* (thinking beings) to *Homo sapiens sapiens* (beings who use language). Because of these advances in our hardware, we are more capable of being cocreators, rather than mere victims or spectators of life's trajectory.

Computer software has also developed. Think of all the apps you can download even to your cell phone: GPS systems, e-mail capabilities, and so on. And human cultures have changed because of travel, expanding and shared knowledge, technology, and science, as well as the communications media, although not always for the better.

Computer hardware can suffer damage, and computer software is susceptible to viruses that can utterly cripple it. And so it is with human hardware, which ages and is subject to injury and death; and with human software, which is constantly bombarded with the deadly viruses of propaganda and consumption-crazy brainwashing. The key to happiness is to honor the body and develop it mindfully but not *identify* with it. Remember, the body is a space suit, while you are the astronaut, the soul who is on safari on planet Earth. You have come here for a purpose; do not allow numbing cultural messages to obscure that purpose—for example, through the serenading by the greedy purveyors of possessions. Human culture is the environment in which you live out your mission, but it should never set your direction.

How We Lose Our Mission

Culture is a double-edged sword. It is one part socializing agent, bringing children into conformity with the norms, and one part propaganda machine, indoctrinating them into groupthink. It wants us to fit neatly under the center of the bell curve, and it punishes those who don't. The ones who fail to keep the rules are locked up as criminals, and the prophets who attempt to lead the evolution are killed as unpatriotic dissidents.

Society is like a snail walking along a meterstick, with its antennae at the 8-centimeter mark, its body and shell at the 5-centimeter mark, and its tail at the 2-centimeter mark. If it keeps walking, at some stage its tail will eventually reach the place where its antennae used to be. It is making progress. But society finds change upsetting and tries to maintain the status quo. It resorts to pithy, simplistic, and tempting cosmologies that assure us that we can be happy *only* if we:

- Continually seek pleasure by feeding the craving to consume.

- Avoid pain at all costs.

- Try harder to be in perfect alignment with the icons of success: fame, power, and riches.

That's our Western culture. But all over the world are cultural rules for living that can influence or limit our mission:

- Cultures that limit the roles of women

- Communitarian cultures that emphasize the needs of family and community over the individual, and vice versa

- Cultures emphasizing eye-for-eye justice and revenge

Anybody following such cultural operating manuals is signing up for a lifetime of frustration. Such a person will neither advance the culture nor find personal happiness. Instead, the culture will fragment and stagnate, and the individual will feel like a failure for being unable to find happiness using the "infallible" tools offered by the culture.

How culture shapes our choices and life direction is very similar to the role of a football coach. Each player on the team has some unique skill set that the coach should try to optimize. Unfortunately, the coach often provides a generic set of rules and strategies about how to play football that has nothing to do with an individual player's actual talents. The player is told on each play, "Run right…, run left…" But the play calls don't match the player's abilities, and in the end, the game is lost.

As with the losing players, most people are sad, frustrated, and unfulfilled in life. But when they attempt to

44

alter the game plan, the coach (culture) says, "No! This is not how it's supposed to be. You're just not trying hard enough!" So we go out and try harder, only to find ourselves less and less happy. Our cultural coaching ignores our sense of pain and failure and just keeps demanding more of our depleted resources.

Look around you: The game plan doesn't seem to be working for most people you know. It doesn't seem to be working for humans as a species. It doesn't even seem to be working for the planet itself. Humanity has become a team that regularly finishes the season at the bottom of the Happiness League.

There are some seven billion people who accept the game plan and live unhappily ever after. And then there are the few who march to a different drumbeat and find serenity, tranquility, and peace. Do you know some of these people?

So, why do we keep renewing the coach's contract and slavishly following an ineffective game plan? Isn't it time to fire the coach? To devise a new game plan?

Critique the Cultural Message

This is where *you* come in. What do you think life is? Is it a random, meaningless farce against which we rail and then drown our grief in our consumer addictions? What if you were not sent here merely to anesthetize your spirit with "bread and circuses," as a cynical Roman poet said some two thousand years ago of the misled populace? What if the game plan that advocates "Avoid pain, pursue pleasure" is the very reason why we keep finishing last in the league? What if you are here for a purpose? A *real* purpose. A purpose that you can easily figure out.

Have you ever thought that maybe you should honor your own misgivings? That maybe the coaching is pathetic and the game plan unworkable?

EXERCISE: Your Coaching

Examine five main tenets—or rules for living—of the "coaching" you've received from family, schooling, religion, mass media, and politicians. For each tenet ask yourself: *How has this contributed to my journey? Has it liberated me or crippled me?* Which cultural messages, rules, or mores have supported your life purpose? Are there cultural messages that have helped you set a life direction that feels good to you? What cultural messages (coaching) seem to take you further from your mission? What cultural influences have pulled you in directions where you feel unhappy or unfulfilled?

5

WHAT LOVE IS:
OUR SHARED
MISSION

Our shared mission here is to love. But love that comes easily provides few learning opportunities. On this planet, we must find a way to love despite hormones, peptides, neurotransmitters, and all the hardwired reactions in the human body. We must learn a love that sees through pain—our own and others—a love that acts with kindness even when our brains are stoked with rage or fear, screaming that we should attack or run. The question, of course, is how? How do we learn this most difficult form of love?

The Anatomy of Love

At its root, "love" is just a word. And that word can have many meanings. Some people define love simply as an emotion or a strong attraction or a sexual bond. Some regard it as a compassionate attitude or a deep acceptance.

Psychologist Erich Fromm, who wrote *The Art of Loving*, contended that love is made of four elements: knowledge, care, responsibility, and respect. Each element may have associated feelings, but love is always about *behavior*. It is active. It does things. It influences the world.

Love begins with *knowledge*: the commitment to understand another being. This includes the skills of asking, listening, and opening—without resistance or defense—to the unique needs and feelings of someone else.

You cannot love without seeing clearly. But the commitment to know the other person means facing inevitable barriers. It's hard to ask and be open when another's pain seems to indict us, make us feel wrong or bad. It's difficult to listen when we are protecting ourselves by using judgments and blame.

Love is more than the connection of one human to another. We are also here to love and know this planet: the creatures, trees, and rocks. This means paying attention to what supports or damages ecological balance. It means learning enough about planetary health to see what's needed in our own backyard.

Care is the commitment to kindness. It's any act that supports the well-being of another—or the Earth itself. Acts of caring must transcend our personal pain—and all of the ways in which we numb or manage that pain—in order to reach across the divide between one being and another.

Responsibility is the act of watching over someone like a good parent. It is the commitment to notice when that person hurts or is in need. But responsibility requires more than mere observing. It is the commitment to protect and somehow join the ones we love in their struggles.

The responsibilities of love can extend to the planet: its creatures, habitats, and ecosystems. Love confers a sense of belonging—to our families and communities, to every living being who is seeking the way, and to the universe itself. This belonging spawns a shared responsibility in which each of us, in some small way, watches over the world.

Respect grows from seeing the innate worth of what we love. All that we say and do should convey a reverence for the beauty and specialness of the other. But when we are hurt or threatened, we protect ourselves with contempt. Pain makes us strip the other of value. Love disappears with each demeaning word or thought.

Respect—whether for a child, a friend, a stranger on the street, or even a steep cascade on some swiftly moving river—is an act of love. And respect is always expressed in action: a touch, a smile, the effort to really listen, a moment of full attention.

Our shared mission here—where things are often so hard and our impulse is to shield ourselves from pain—comes down to four things:

- See the other.

- Be kind to the other.

- Protect the other.

- Find the worth in the other.

These are the actions that make a relationship *I and thou*; they are the anatomy of love. This is what we came to learn.

How you enact love is a life's work. Likely, it is the journey of many lives. To see, to be kind, to protect, and to find the other's value is our purpose. And to do it while we hurt—while we yearn to drink, or shut or rage away that hurt; while the other grows small and broken with pain and from all the ways he or she avoids pain—is the work of life.

Part 2

PURPOSE: WHAT YOUR LIFE IS TELLING YOU

6

LIFE PURPOSE
MEDITATION

Every one of us has the potential to create an experience called *wise mind*. Wise mind is not where you practice reason and logic. And it doesn't involve your emotions. Wise mind is a state of awareness where you can find your personal truth, where deep, intuitive knowledge shows up in simple, clear thoughts and images. Because wise mind gives access to knowledge that your conscious mind may not have, it's a good place to seek information about your mission here.

For many people, life purpose may be discovered without using reason and conscious seeking. It is a sense of who you are and why you're here that comes from the very center of the mystery of breath and awareness.

WISE MIND MEDITATION

To reach the state of wise mind, you can do the following meditation:

1. Focus your eyes on a single object, or just close them.

2. Breathe into your center, where your diaphragm moves, just beneath your sternum. Focus your attention on the breath going to this spot.

3. Breathe at a normal depth and pace.

4. Say to yourself *in* on the in-breath and *out* as you exhale.

5. When thoughts arise, just say to yourself *thought* and return your attention to the breath at your center.

6. If emotions or physical sensations show up, notice them and return your attention to the breath at your center.

7. When your attention drifts for any reason, return it to the breath.

8. Continue to watch your breath for three to five minutes.

Don't worry about intrusive thoughts, sensations, or other distractions. They're natural. They will go on happening, even though you may notice that your mind slows down a bit. The goal isn't to stop thoughts and distractions but, as soon as you notice your mind drifting, to return your attention to your breath. In the course of a few minutes, you'll get distracted and go back to your breath a good number of times. That's fine; you'll get to wise mind anyway.

Using Wise Mind

In the state of wise mind, you can ask questions that may be answered with a suddenly clear thought or image. Or you can do what we will suggest now: use a guided visualization that leads toward the truth you're seeking and allows room for wise mind to provide answers in the form of an image or "sudden knowing." Use the following "Life Purpose Meditation" *after* you have spent three to five minutes getting into wise mind. You can:

- Record it, including lots of pauses to give you time to notice experiences that come up. Simply close your eyes and turn on the recording after several minutes of breathing into your center.

- Have a trusted individual read it to you.

- Read it yourself, pausing to close your eyes and visualize the images after each paragraph.

LIFE PURPOSE MEDITATION

Take a breath…into your heart, your center. Bring your attention to that place. Every breath deepens your connection—to the center of your body, the source of life. This is the place where you know what is most important, where you remember all the lessons you have learned.

Make a space now at the center…the source. You can imagine it as a clearing in a lush forest—a meadow of grass and moss in sun and shadow. This is the place to wait, to watch and listen. Find a spot where you can rest and be still. It might be a hollow in the ground, or a stump or rock to lean against.

Settle in now to the place you've chosen and listen to whatever you hear. Watch whatever catches your eye: a branch moving in the wind, the grass moving. In time, if you listen and watch long enough, something will show up in the clearing. It may come through the trees or out of the sky, or it may just appear. Don't force it or try to make something happen. Just wait for as long as it takes.

Whatever visits you is safe and means only the best for you. Whenever it comes, it will bring a message—something you've been waiting to know about your purpose, what you came here to do in this life. You may recognize whatever comes as a symbol, or it may just carry the message to you as a sudden knowing—an awareness.

You have only to wait in the clearing. Let time pass and be patient. But stay alert, because the visit could come at any time.

What Did You Learn?

At the end of the meditation, you are encouraged to wait in the clearing. Keep your eyes closed and hold on to the image of the meadow. Give yourself time to let emerge whatever wise mind gives you. If an image comes up, ask what it symbolizes. What does the image represent? If you have the experience of "sudden knowing," let it crystallize and become more clear to you. Let this awareness grow, take shape. Ask what it means: what you need to be doing in your life *now*, what direction you should be heading, and what opportunities you should pay attention to.

Let what you learned from the "Life Purpose Meditation" settle in. Take several days to process it, returning again and again to the images or insights. And ask yourself this question: *What would I be doing now if I were living my life purpose?*

7

WISE MIND

We spend much of our lives in problem-solving mode. We are captives of what will happen next: the next problem and its solution, the next challenge, the next danger and its remedy. Our days are a series of events that must be planned for, coped with. They require us to be forever leaning forward, looking beyond the present moment so that we can bring order to an uncertain future.

Our lives are problems and solutions: *How can I go to the bank during lunch hour and still get something to eat? What do I do at the gym if my knee hurts? The car is burning oil; how much for a new one? How do I explain my dropping sales numbers? Should I go back to school? Is it too cold to walk to work?* A mind locked in problem solving loses perspective. All we can see is the next difficulty, the next broken thing. And a fog descends on our days, obscuring the forks and crossroads, covering all but the next step.

If the work of problem-solving mind is to fix things, the work of wise mind is to see the moments of choice—not about buying a car or how to spin bad sales numbers, but choices about *how to live*. Wise mind sees what is lost in the fog of days—those forks and crossroads where we can set off in a chosen direction. Wise mind intuitively knows our mission and understands each choice as an opportunity to move toward or away from life purpose.

The problem of the old oil burner isn't the province of wise mind. Rather, it is the question of spending your resources on what you truly care about. A drop in sales numbers is unfortunate, but wise mind asks, *Do I care about what I'm selling, and does this job in any way feel meaningful?*

The fog of days will not lift as you struggle to solve the next problem. It will hang like a lowland mist, close to the ground. In order to see the real choices embedded in your problems, and the opportunities to act on your mission that show up every day, you'll have to climb—up beyond fixes and solutions—to wise mind.

Wise Mind Every Day

In the "Life Purpose Meditation," we suggested the use of wise mind as a platform to investigate a specific question: *What is my mission here?* But you can use wise mind as a daily pathfinder, a way to orient toward your purpose as you start each morning.

Think about your usual routine: the alarm goes off and you begin thinking about all the challenges of the day—and what to do about them. You start preparing and solving. An alternative, or at least an additional process, could be a wise mind meditation. The steps of inducing wise mind were discussed in the last chapter, but now we'll show how wise mind can help you recognize and meet each moment of choice in your day.

MEDITATION FOR GUIDANCE

Every morning, soon after you wake up, do this brief meditation:

1. Focus on your center, that spot just beneath your sternum, and breathe into that place.

2. Say to yourself *in* on the in-breath and *out* as you exhale.

3. Keep your attention on your breath. If thoughts intrude, say to yourself **thought** and refocus on your breath.

4. Let the rhythm of your breathing be all there is for a minute or two.

5. Now ask this question: **Today what are the choices that matter?** Scan your planned events.

6. Don't try to answer with your rational mind. Reason and logic won't help. Let your intuitive, wise mind respond. Wait for the answer.

7. Ask one more thing: **How can I act on my life purpose today?**

8. Now keep focusing on the breath. And let the answer arrive in its own time. It may come as a specific thought or an image, or it may arrive as a moment of recognition during your day.

9. Continue observing your breath until you feel ready to stop. Remember that the answer may show up during your meditation or much later.

As always during a meditation, intrusive thoughts, sensations, and other distractions are natural. The goal isn't to stop them, but to keep returning to your breath while opening to deep knowledge and wisdom. Remember that, each day, your answers may be different. This is because each day *is* different, with its own moments of choice. So let your wise mind guide you even before you rise in the morning. Planning and problem solving are reasonable things. But seeing your day through the lens of life purpose makes possible a real clarity.

8

WHAT YOUR GIFTS AND ATTRIBUTES TELL YOU ABOUT YOUR LIFE PURPOSE

When Neil Armstrong landed on the moon in July 1969, he was wearing a space suit that had taken millions of dollars and lots of time and human ingenuity to develop. His space suit had to do two things: first, protect him from the lunar environment and, second, enable him to perform his tasks.

We are souls on a mission to planet Earth. We have come here to learn and grow. Like space travelers, we need equipment that is appropriate for the world in which we find ourselves. And, like Armstrong's space suit, we are built to allow the fulfillment of our mission or life purpose.

In this metaphor Neil Armstrong is to his space suit as the soul is to the body, mind, and emotions. Armstrong drives the space suit, just as the soul drives the process of incarnation. The modern human has all of the upgrades of our evolutionary past built in: from our single-celled origins to mammalian emotions to our ability to think (*Homo sapiens*). So let's do a quick check of this equipment.

Your Mission Equipment

What mission equipment is in your backpack? What features does your space suit have to enable your purpose? In this chapter we will suggest that there are various kinds of equipment: physical, emotional, and intellectual attributes, as well as desires, values, and talents. Then we will help you see that you have a very unique configuration of these features, that this uniqueness—your talents—is the key to figuring out your mission, and, finally, that vocation is where your mission meets your daily life.

Physical talents. Humans are found in a huge range of environments, from Arctic wastelands to tropical jungles. We have invented all kinds of games and engaged in all kinds of work. The result has been the development of physical skills that are truly amazing. From Jesse Owens, who won four gold medals in the 1936 Olympics, to Michael Jordan, who seemed to defy gravity on the basketball court, sports, leisure activities, and work have provided outlets for the actualization of dreams.

How are you gifted in this arena? Good looks? Athleticism? Strength? Great hand-eye coordination? Great energy or stamina? Good health?

Emotional qualities. We inherited emotions from the mammals. The mammals, who arrived on the scene about two hundred million years ago, developed the limbic system that allowed them to dream and emote and raise their young. The reptiles, who existed long before the mammals, did not have emotions or dream or spend any time with their offspring. Over millions of years, these emotions have expanded to include virtues like courage, empathy, love, joy, lightheartedness, tenderness, and compassion. These were the hallmark of such giants as Mother Teresa and Gandhi, and marked their mission and self-prescribed purpose.

Which of these emotions move *you* the most? If you were to build a life purpose, which of them would define your mission?

Intellectual skills. These include creativity, problem solving, self-reflection, and abstract thought, all of which can be applied to any worthwhile pursuit: mathematics, music, literature, research. History is replete with examples, such as Copernicus, Newton, Pasteur, and Einstein, whose intellectual talent gave direction to their life purpose and alerted them to their mission.

Where do you find *your* mind wanting to focus? What special intellectual interest and capacity do you have? Who are the thinkers and what are the ideas that have inspired you?

Desires, interests, and preferences. We are as much products of the future as we are of history. Desires, interests, and preferences beckon us as strongly as our past actions push us. They are important factors in helping us figure out a life purpose. Of how many successful people have you heard it said, "He always wanted to be..." Desires can either augment physical, emotional, or intellectual gifts or compensate for deficits. For instance, recently a friend related a story of an encounter on a train with a young man who had been struck by cerebral palsy so that his legs were pencil thin. However, his desire to be a long-distance runner was so strong that he regularly took part in marathons, using crutches and a very highly developed upper body to complete the course, and beat many normal runners each time.

What ignites that kind of energy in you? Forget about the possible impediments for now and focus on the desire itself.

Values. These serve as the basic GPS system of our actions. They are different from our ideals (which is how we would like to act). For example, your ideal probably is that you ought never to tell a lie, but this may be overridden, on occasion, when the value of being well thought of trumps that ideal and "forces" you to dissimulate.

Values provide an accurate map of how we are likely to behave in any given situation. In the stormy sea of conflicting paradigms, they hold the ship of your life steadily on course. But this course can be a healthy or unhealthy one. So it is important to examine your values. Moving steadily in the wrong direction is going to take you farther from your intended destination than standing still is. In the next chapter, we will offer you an exercise to examine and change some of your values.

EXERCISE: Identifying Your Strengths

Using the five items in the previous list (physical talents; emotional qualities; intellectual skills; desires, interests, and preferences; and values), write down your particular strengths or attributes, and using a scale from 1 to 3, rate how important each one is to you. This will give you important data about your possible mission and life purpose.

Taken together, these parts constitute what you have in your tool kit when you parachute into incarnation.

The Creativity of Nature

Nature gives you particular tools just because you are a member of the human species. But, like a talented artist, nature never paints the same picture twice. So you are a *unique* human, with a unique combination of human attributes and a unique purpose in the cosmos. You must unearth your uniqueness and discover your purpose. Let's use language as a metaphor.

Language and accent are an interesting analogy, because although there are shared speech patterns that make you identifiable as a member of a language group (for example, a speaker of English) or even as a member of a subgroup of English speakers (Americans) or even as a sub-subgroup (Americans who speak English with an Alabama accent), there are also unique qualities that identify you as an *individual* within that group; for example, "Oh, that is Joseph speaking!"

Similarly, each species speaks its own "language"; by this we mean that it has its own attributes that identify it as a species. But each individual within that species speaks this language in its own unique way (has its own unique constellation of variations of the attributes that the entire species shares). It's the particular configuration (not the attributes per se) that makes you who you are, so the *configuration* is the clue to your unique contribution, mission, and passion.

Four Simple Metaphors

The English language has twenty-six letters, just twenty-six. And yet the combined works of Shakespeare are created from these twenty-six symbols. You, too, though built of basic human qualities, are a unique piece of literature.

Western music is built on a seven-note scale, just seven notes. And yet all of Bach's music is created from these seven notes. You, too, though built of basic human qualities, are a unique piece of music.

DNA is composed of four nucleotides (adenine, cytosine, thymine, and guanine), only four. Yet all seven billion human beings are built from instructions encoded using just these molecules.

Computer language is based on Boolean algebra, a simple binary code consisting of two elements: 0 and 1, just two symbols. And yet everything you read, hear, and see on your computer screen is built from these two symbols. You, too, though built of basic human qualities, are a unique piece of divine computing.

Why the Uniqueness?

Individuals, then, come to planet Earth in all kinds of configurations, permutations, and combinations of these basic attributes. That is precisely what will equip each one for a *unique* mission or life purpose.

The question then becomes, Why did *you* show up with this unique configuration of attributes? Can it be because you are on a previously agreed-upon mission for which that particular constellation gave you the ideal resources? What a pity if you were to keep these gifts locked in the closet of your unconscious.

Talents

Your talents are the innate skills that nature gave you to realize your uniqueness, but you are to use them in the service of life. You are a mail carrier with a bunch of letters in your bag, but although the letters are in *your* bag, they do not belong to you. Rather they belong to the people whose names are on the envelopes. Your job, your unique privilege, is to deliver them to the owners. The greatest happiness comes from this realization of service. Try to hold on to the letters and you'll get fired.

By this we mean that since all missions (from that of the cosmos itself to your particular mission) are woven into the same divine plan, our talents are not meant for narcissistic self-glorification. Each gift you come with was given to you to share with the community of life on planet Earth. And while you are fully entitled to make a good living from the exercise of your talents, you are not meant to make a killing from them. There are, then, two ways to waste talents: bury them by not developing or even employing them, on the one hand, and use them simply to hoard fame or fortune, on the other hand.

EXERCISE: Putting Your Strengths to Use

Review the strengths or attributes you listed in the previous exercise. And consider the mail-carrier metaphor. Where do these talents need to be "delivered"? Your unique mission is supported by your unique collection of attributes (space-suit equipment). Next to each listed attribute, write something about where or how you are (or could be) using it.

Mission vs. Vocation

There is an important distinction between mission and vocation. Mission is never about the job we do, the profession we're in, the relationships we have. Rather, it is about the cultivation of some virtue or virtues, such as compassion, courage, patience, forgiveness, or resilience. Therefore, vocation or calling or profession must always be in the service of mission, not the other way around. You're not here to *be* a farmer or a politician; you've chosen to be a farmer or a politician in order to align with your mission and grow. If, for instance, you choose the development of courage as a mission, it might be possible for you to do that as a lion tamer, as a soldier, or as an advocate for the homeless. Your unique combination of attributes will help you decide among these possible professions.

To summarize, all of us come with the same basic equipment or attributes, but we each have unique variations on these attributes. Talents are those attributes wherein we shine or are especially gifted. Values will nudge these talents to find expression in a particular kind of mission, and vocation or profession will be the ideal outlet for that mission in the form of service to the planet. So you, dear reader, have come to planet Earth with a space suit that has all of the features that humans need, but your particular variations on these features are utterly unique. In some of these features, not only will you be unique, but you will also *shine*; and these features we call talents. But what are you going to do with these talents? Here is where your values come in. Your values will point you toward focusing on particular virtues (your mission)—for example, courage, compassion, or patience—and then you will seek a profession, vocation, or avocation that provides the ideal outlet for developing and exercising that mission as service.

9

WHAT YOUR VALUES
TELL YOU ABOUT
YOUR LIFE PURPOSE

There's a Sufi legend about a group of travelers who set out across the barren desert from their hometown; let's call it Old Town. Their objective was to arrive at New Town, which was many hundreds of miles away. They were told that if they kept going due east, they would find a major crossroad with a great wooden signpost pointing in four directions, one of which would be toward New Town.

They traveled for weeks until both tempers and supplies were wearing thin. They were convinced they were lost. They grumbled and debated about whether or not to turn back, but just then, one of them spotted a cross-road up ahead in the shimmering haze of the desert. They eagerly ran forward, only to find that the signpost had fallen down in a great dust storm. They began to weep and wail over their inevitable demise. Then one of the group, an old man, said, "We are not lost. Stand the signpost upright; the four pointers are still attached to the main post." They did so. Then he said, "Now twist it around until the pointer that says Old Town is pointing back along the route from which we have come." Again, they did so. "Now," said the old man, "I think you can see clearly the direction in which the New Town pointer is pointing."

In other words, the best chance you have of finding your future is to examine your past. And that is what we will help you do in this chapter, which is about values and ideals.

Differentiating Values from Ideals

There is a subtle but very important difference between values and ideals. Cultures of all kinds, whether they be religions, nations, or families, aver that they are guided by ideals—the highest aspirations, such as love, peace, harmony, and the Golden Rule—but their behavior frequently belies that assertion. Religions engage in inquisitions, nations engage in conquests, and families engage in vendettas. What *actually* drives their behavior are their values, for example, being orthodox (in the case of religions), being powerful (in the case of nations), and getting even (in the case of families). So, we frequently find that the *values* of power, privilege, wealth, and so on trump the *ideals* of love, peace, and harmony. Therefore, you must learn to distinguish between the ideals you have heard espoused and the values you have seen exemplified in your culture.

Let's expand on this very important difference. In 1776 the US Founding Fathers created an inspiring document that stated, as an *ideal*, that "...all men are created equal...," but in fact, they lived in or even promoted a society whose *values* enslaved black people, regarded women and children as mere chattels, and called the native population, in that same august document, "savages." American history, gratefully, is the record of those values slowly morphing into the ideals set forth by the Founding Fathers. The very significant decline in violence over the course of human history—in wars, genocides, torture, and slavery, and in abuse of women, children, and animals—is evidence of the steady progress from values to ideals.

But this evolution is more fitful than smooth; it is more like the punctuated equilibria of Stephen Jay Gould than the gradualism of Darwin, because once a significant advance has been achieved, cultures tend to render it divine and, eventually, the forward momentum stagnates in the fixation on tradition. Cultural conservatism tries to herd us tightly under the bell curve, punishing the laggards as lawbreakers and the prophets as troublemakers. But eventually, yesterday's lawbreakers will reach the place where the prophets used to stand. By then, of course, the prophets will have moved farther ahead. This is the journey from mere values to soul-filled ideals.

Mission: Moving from Values to Ideals

Initially, it is charismatic figures like the Buddha, Jesus, Jefferson, Gandhi, and Martin Luther King Jr. who point out the discrepancies between ideals and values, and who then offer us a road map to connect them. Our species-wide mission is to move humanity from a life based on values to a life based on ideals. And the individual purpose dovetails seamlessly with that, by taking one or two virtues of the species-wide transformation and making them a personal mission. When we sign up for an Earth mission, we agree to push the evolutionary process forward by finding a niche (a personal mission). You put your shoulder to one of the wheels of the mud-stuck wagon and help it lurch forward.

The promised land is the full alignment of the ideals and values of the species; the holy grail is the full alignment of the ideals and values of the individual.

Typically, you have, consciously or unconsciously, allowed values to decide your journey up to now. You need to be able to tell values and ideals apart, and then determine if you want to bring them into alignment. Let's use the metaphor of a car ride to represent your life journey. It's the movement of your hands on the steering wheel (your behavior) that determines the route your car is going to take. Ideals are the hand movements that will take you to your *stated* destination, but values are the movements that will take you to your *intended* destination. If your ideals and values are aligned, the stated destination and the intended destination will be the same. For example, the aspiration to forgive becomes the practice of forgiveness. If ideals and values are unaligned, then values (and the intended destination) will win out over ideals (and the stated destination). If you are aligned, then you walk the talk.

So values are the basic GPS system of our actions. They provide an accurate map of how we are likely to behave in any given situation. And this can be a healthy or an unhealthy course. Therefore, it is important to *examine* your values. Moving steadily in the wrong direction will take you farther from your stated destination than standing still will.

Your values will point you toward the mission you agreed to do before you incarnated, but only if you are *awake* and aligned. Your unique configuration of values will direct your choices and shape your goals—in the service of your mission if you are awake, and in the service of the "seek pleasure, avoid pain" agenda if you are asleep.

To summarize, behavior—meaning your thoughts, words, and deeds—is how you *actually* perform in the world. It is the raw data of your living. Your ideals, on the other hand, are how you would be if your behavior were in alignment with your highest aspirations, and your values are the actual determinants of your behavior.

Aligning your values with your ideals, then, is a sine qua non of finding your mission. Therefore, we want to propose an exercise to help you awaken to what your values really are so that you can determine whether they are in harmony with your ideals.

EXERCISE: "The Ten Commandments by Which I Live"

Here is how to do this exercise. Look at the following ten categories:

Work life

Finances

Intimate relationships

Friends and social life

Family

Community and citizenship

Education and learning

Spirituality

Physical self-care

Recreation and leisure

Now write down the value that actually drives your behavior in each category. Don't record your *ideal* behavior in that arena, but what really dictates how you perform there. For example, in the intimate relationships category, your ideal might be "You shall love unconditionally," whereas your value

83

might be "You shall be sure you are treated fairly and get what you deserve." Or in the family category, your ideal might be "You shall put family first," whereas your value may be "You shall not let yourself be taken advantage of."

And to impress on yourself just how much power this value exercises over you, we want you to express it as a commandment; for example, "You shall..." or "You shall not..." For instance, in the area of work, possible commandments might be "You must get promoted and advance," "You must have a good salary," "You should always give your maximum effort," or "You should work at what you love."

When you've completed the list, examine the commandments and ask yourself, *Which of these commandments are hurting me, and which of them are empowering me? Which are in alignment with my ideals, and which are driven by fear or the pleasure-pain agenda? Which result in the happiness derived from doing what matters, and which lead to sadness or exhaustion?*

When you bring these commandments to full consciousness, then you understand what your values really are. Then you are free to change them or develop them further.

Goal Tending

Once values, commandments, and behavior are lined up, you can create goals that, unlike values, are pragmatic plans with achievable objectives. So for each of the previous categories, record one goal and one action item that will help translate the value into a project of self-liberation. And the action item must be measurable. In other words, you must be able to see immediately whether or not you are performing. For example, if your goal is to run a marathon, then the action item might be to join an organization that helps train people to run marathons, rather than a vague idea to improve fitness.

Then put a timeline to it. An example might be this: In the area of intimate relationships, your goal is to improve your communication skills. So your action item might be "Visit a bookstore and find a good book or video on the topic." And your timeline might be "within the next week."

Now go back to the chart you created and attach to each of the ten categories a goal, an action item, and a timeline.

Briefly, in this chapter we have shown that values are not the same as ideals and that we tend to be driven by values more than by ideals. Just as civilizations advance by inculcating ideal-driven values into the culture, so you, too, will be excellently served by morphing your ideals into acted-upon values. A major aspect of your mission is translating your ideals into the values that inform your practical choices and behavior. "The Ten Commandments by Which I Live" exercise helped you to identify many of your values, and you may have seen gaps between your ideals and your values. This is actually good news: every gap gives you an element of what your mission is. Bridging the values-ideals gaps is your mission.

10

WHAT YOUR RECURRING CHALLENGES TELL YOU ABOUT YOUR LIFE PURPOSE

Your particular mission, as we've suggested, is made up of things you'll learn and things you will do. What you seek to learn can usually be described as a virtue or ideal: patience, compassion, truthfulness, awareness (of the needs and pain of others), generosity, courage (in the face of danger or suffering), commitment and determination, temperance and balance, willingness (to feel, rather than run from feelings), and many others.

We learn and develop these virtues through a series of challenges that we may visit many times in the course of a life. If we are asleep and don't learn much from a particular challenge, it will show up again and again, in this life and perhaps others, until the lesson is learned. A challenge that is avoided or resisted damages us. We become more stuck, more dysfunctional. Conversely, a challenge that we actually face, where we find a way to change or grow, brings us into alignment with our purpose. We wake up, and each time the challenge arrives, we meet it more elegantly, more effectively. As time goes on, these challenging vicissitudes become a key to self-liberation—and true happiness.

As an example, consider the experience of a woman who encounters the following challenges:

- Her mother dies, and she faces loneliness and the *fear* of being alone. She begins drinking and seeking comfort from any man who will give her attention.

- In relationship 1, involving a withdrawn, irritable man with whom she feels lonely and judged, she begins using prescription painkillers. She's afraid to leave until she finds...

- Relationship 2, involving a workaholic who falls asleep each night in front of the TV. Again she feels disconnected, but fears leaving and being on her own. She adds a bottle of port each day to multiple painkillers and valium addiction. This man breaks up with her.

- She moves in with her sister, who spends most nights at her boyfriend's house. The loneliness is overwhelming, and so begins...

- Relationship 3, involving a withdrawn, critical man with a marijuana addiction.

Notice how the same challenge keeps showing up: loneliness and the fear of being alone. And the response is also the same: find someone and numb away the pain. The lesson never gets learned. She continues to seek relief across so many painful relationships—rather than seeking the *courage* to be alone or the *willingness* to face fear.

It may take many more challenges, well beyond a single lifetime, before these lessons are taken in.

Consider also the case of a high-tech entrepreneur who developed and sold (along with his patents) three companies over fifteen years. "It's a storybook life," he says, "except for all the sickness around me."

- His mother died of cancer when he was seventeen.

- His sister developed bipolar disorder in college and has lost jobs and relationships during multiple manic episodes.

- His first wife developed postpartum depression, which led to divorce when he resented and resisted her demands for more help with the baby.

- His second wife hid from him that she had Crohn's disease until after they were married. She was hospitalized twice in the last year and has required extensive use of steroids. "They make her high as a kite and then depressed," he says. "I can't stand it."

- Four months ago he was diagnosed with a degenerative condition of the spine.

The entrepreneur has slept through each of his challenges; he hasn't gotten it. As each loved one got sick, he withdrew and abandoned the person to her pain. He thinks it's unfair, that he's been "screwed by life." But really, he's being given new opportunities to learn an old lesson. So far it has cost two marriages and resulted in a deepening sense of failure. Finally, the challenge arrives in the form of his own health catastrophe. He now must learn the lessons of generosity and compassion for pain through his own suffering.

Origin of Life Challenges

In each lifetime we attract the challenges we need to develop as souls. If we embrace them and work with them, then every event and every relationship will be grist for the mill of our growth. If we avoid the challenge and try to hide from the pain, we are literally *creating* the next problem. When the woman who was afraid to be alone ran to another broken, disconnected man, she was creating her next drama: a new person who would inflict the old emotional hunger. When our entrepreneur withdrew from the needs of those around him, he inevitably entered a new relationship where, once again, he had to face human need and human pain.

On some level we are drawn to situations that offer us a chance to grow. The person who's afraid may seek dangers to confront that fear. A person who is self-centered may find people in need to be like magnets, endlessly pulling for a collision between the yearnings of self and others. The person who is driven by self-righteous beliefs will often struggle with individuals who are full of the same angry certainty. And the traditional solution—putting an opponent in the philosophical crosshairs—merely plants seeds for the next conflict.

So the challenges keep coming. And the answer is not in running away. The pain we avoid works its way back to us. The pain we avoid drives us from one cliff to another, from one lost chance to the next reenactment of our central drama.

At what point do you say, *Enough? I have played out this scene a dozen different times, and it is always the same. I do what I've always done, and things evolve as they inevitably do.* When do you question not the challenge itself, but your old, traditional response? Perhaps, simply, you say *Enough* when you recognize that this struggle has happened before and that how you cope has taken you always to the same stuck place.

The first step to changing, therefore, is recognizing the familiarity of the challenge, seeing that it has come before. And the second step is identifying the lesson embedded in this painful struggle. What is it trying to teach you?

EXERCISE: What Themes Run through Your Challenges?

List the major challenges in your life: situations that were difficult or painful, and that required you to make a choice. Now look for common themes. Which challenges touched on similar issues or content? Which pushed you to the same emotional place? Which triggered a similar response?

Now, for challenges that were thematically similar, ask yourself what they might be trying to teach. Is there a lesson that could be common to these situations? What didn't work about how you responded? Did you find, at times, a response that fared better? Which virtue or ideal describes what these situations require, what they demand of you?

Now step back. Many of these challenges came to you for a reason. They are part of your purpose, your mission here. What do they tell you about your mission? If each challenge were a spoke on a wheel and they were all connected to a central hub, what would that tell you about the core issue from which they all spring?

11

THE SIX PATHS

This chapter is a condensed version of material from *The Six Pathways of Destiny* by Ralph Metzner (El Verano, CA: Green Earth Foundation, 2012).

The discovery of our life purpose starts with seeing the path that we are now on—and what that path reveals about our reason for coming here. Before our birth, we already had an intention or vision for this life: what we came here to do and be. The ancient Zen koan "What was your original face before you were born?" relates to this plan. We carry an intuitive sense of the vision. And throughout our lives, we may get glimpses in the form of dreams, yearnings, attractions, and sudden insights, as well as through teachers or role models who inspire us along the way.

In this life are six great archetypal pathways (chosen individually but more often in combination) that can help us express our talents and realize our mission: the teacher/communicator, the healer/peacemaker, the warrior/guardian, the explorer/scientist, the builder/organizer, and the artist/designer. We'll talk more about these six directions for life purpose in a moment, but first, some history.

In traditional societies, the role you were to play was predetermined by the family you were born into and could not be changed. In ancient India, for example, the principle of dharma meant that you were born into one of four basic castes: the warrior/ruler, the priest/teacher, the merchant/trader, or the laborer/servant. In medieval times in Japan, four walks of life were recognized: the way of the knight, the farmer, the artisan, and the merchant. In medieval Europe there was a similar division into four orders: knights/nobles, peasants/serfs, priests/monks, and merchants/traders. Whereas the landowning aristocracy and land-working peasantry and slaves were locked into their roles by family heredity, the religious orders and merchant guilds afforded a little more choice and mobility.

None of the roles in ancient or medieval societies made much room for women. So women were often required to express their life missions by developing specific roles *inside* a family.

The Industrial Revolution, of course, reordered society, slowly creating space for an expanding middle class and a movement toward gender equality. The six life paths, for many, are no longer blocked or dictated by gender and lineage. They can be chosen, sought. These directions can now reflect our chosen purpose and mission, rather than our predetermined fate.

Karma, Fate, and Destiny

In the past-life and interlife research we reviewed earlier, it's clear that souls *choose* to incarnate in their successive lifetimes as personalities. These selections are made, with the support of guides, from a number of options.

The choice of a particular life always involves two key elements: karma or fate, and destiny. Karma is based on past-life choices and the current vector of our souls' development. We may be working on issues such as independence, empathy, or kindness; we may be developing the ability to nourish and take care of others, the willingness to be steadfast and keep commitments, or the ability to build and create. Karma isn't punishment or being forced to relive past mistakes. It's the lesson plan for what we're trying to learn in *this* life, and a path to rectify choices from past lives.

Karma or fate includes the genetic threads of ancestry and family, of place and culture, of gifts and liabilities. Fate—from the Latin *fata*, "what has been decreed"—is the unavoidable, fixed precondition of our existence, the cards we have been dealt in this round of life on planet Earth. In the Greek myth of the three *Moirai*, sisters of time and fate, *Lachesis* is the one who "dispenses the lots," and thus determines the conditions into which the new life is to be born. We know that as souls, we chose these conditions ourselves to foster growth. But once chosen, they are our lot, immutable preconditions of a particular life.

Destiny, on the other hand, is about the future. It's what we choose to be and do with all that we've been allotted, how we play out the role—with its possibilities and limitations—that we've accepted.

Fate and destiny always interweave. Each of us is born with a certain gender, with a particular constitution, traits and talents, strengths and weaknesses. We have chosen to be born into the particular social and historical conditions of our families. These are all matters of fate, the starting point of each new life we will live. What we make of it, how we respond to the obstacles and challenges of our fated origin—these are the open-ended potentials of our destiny.

Fate and destiny are midwives to the birth of our particular life purpose. Each of the six paths is not only a career or direction, our work in the world, but also, at a deeper level, our destiny, the way we are seeking to learn and grow. Let's look at each of the six paths in turn.

The Way of the Teacher/ Communicator

In ancient times and in indigenous cultures, the epic storyteller was also the teacher and spiritual guide, passing on the oral traditions of the tribe. The elders told stories to the younger generation in order to instill in them both moral and practical knowledge. These were the memory keepers, holders of the collective wisdom of an entire community. An example is Hawaiian kahuna elder Hale Makua, who described being trained to remember the names, voyages, and teachings of more than twenty generations of his royal ancestors.

In modern times this path—holder and teacher of knowledge—is exemplified by the historian, biographer, journalist, academic, schoolteacher, philosopher, and virtually anyone who communicates what is known. The passing of knowledge to those who do not yet have it is a function that can accompany all the other paths as well. This work has great importance, regardless of whether the teaching is done at home with one's child or in the halls of the academy.

Teachers, whether ancient storytellers or modern journalists, whether parents or professors, do something critical: they name things. Social disorder results from the failure to see, understand, and deal with reality— the failure to call things by their proper names. An example is the recent Supreme Court decision finding that corporations should be accorded the same rights as people. A strong corrective response from many points on the political spectrum said, "Corporations are *not* people." Confucian thinkers referred to this function as "the rectification of names": saying what things actually are, the truth.

Teachers do this. They are here to remind us of what is really true.

The Way of the Healer/Peacemaker

From Hippocrates to wise witches, shamans, midwives, and herbalists, and from Chinese acupuncturists to Indian practitioners of ayurveda, homeopaths, and holistic and allopathic MDs, the path of the healer has had a great variety of travelers—and many specialties: physical medicine, surgery, osteopathy, spiritual healing, bodywork, psychotherapy, mindfulness training and yoga, and even veterinarian medicine, to name a few.

There are also the healers of the planet: ecologists and conservationists who practice sustainable lifeways through permaculture, soil restoration and organic food growing, protection of our water, reduction of environmental toxins, preservation of wetlands, and hundreds of other initiatives.

There are healers of society, who balance and reconcile conflicted families, groups, communities, and nations. They teach nonviolent communication and work for social justice. They are the Gandhis and the Mandelas; they are the parents who teach children to share instead of fight; they are the ones, in gatherings all over the world, who seek common ground and shared solutions.

The path of healing and peacemaking can touch many—such as have Doctors Without Borders and the

Truth and Reconciliation Commission in South Africa—or a single person in pain. Scale doesn't matter; the path itself means everything.

The Way of the Warrior/Guardian

This is the pathway of those who protect. In the warrior traditions, such as the samurai in Japan or the knightly orders of medieval Europe, there was always an oath of allegiance to a chieftain and a deity. The oath signaled a life-or-death commitment of the warrior to protect his community. In modern times the warrior—whether a member of the police, judiciary, or military—still takes an oath to protect.

But the warrior/guardian path has far more roles than for those who bear arms. True warriors include attorneys who fight for justice, whistle-blowers and reformers who battle corruption, public health officials who struggle to contain disease, and social activists who protect the exploited. Thus, the warrior protects the community from both outside invasion and internal corruption.

By extension, warriors also include athletes who channel society's aggression into competitions and mock battles, as well as captains of commerce who fiercely compete to protect territory and market share.

As with other paths, the warrior can operate at many levels: from defending one's country in violent battle to defending one's home from predatory lenders or one's child from a flawed school system. The nobility of the guardian path derives from the willingness to be vigilant and to fight so that others may be safe.

The Way of the Explorer/Scientist

This is the path of those who seek to expand knowledge. They seek to discover the previously unknown, to unravel the mysteries of the natural world, to identify the hidden lawful causes behind observable phenomena. Einstein once suggested that the most beautiful thing we can experience is the mysterious—and that this is the source of science.

While explorers, those who sail or trek to new lands, have been part of human development from the beginning, and sciences such as astronomy date back to ancient cultures, the scientific revolution in the sixteenth and seventeenth centuries changed this path forever. It provided a reliable method for observing and collecting data, testing hypotheses, and building theories.

The path of the explorer/scientist has many branches: medical, social, and psychological exploration; research into the properties of the Earth and the Universe; the artifacts of ancient civilizations; and many more. From drilling to discover the secrets of deep, ancient lakes in Antarctica to learning why your child gets so angry at dinner, this path is always about asking and answering questions, particularly the question, Why? Explorers push the boundary of what is known, whether by the individual or by all humankind. The drive to hike toward the beauty of a remote lake is no less the path of explorer than the work of Jonas Salk, developer of the polio vaccine.

The Way of the Builder/Organizer

This is the direction for those who make things. Historically, this was the pathway for farmers, herders, and gardeners; for miners, smiths, and metallurgists; for masons, carpenters, and engineers. Today the path is taken by those who build our infrastructure, provide transportation, and may spend their weekends doing home improvement. It is shared by laborers, bus drivers, and certainly homemakers, who choose carefully (for beauty and usefulness) the elements and arrangement of every room.

Those who create businesses, who develop and make products, and who organize events and entertainment all follow this path. Also in this category is the union or neighborhood organizer who organizes recreational and interest groups and even the block-party coordinator.

Builders help form the world, physically and socially. On any scale they shape our lives—the buildings and roads we use, the groups we belong to.

The Way of the Artist/Designer

This final path is for those who create. Art has long been associated with the nine traditional Greek muses. Three of them (Calliope, Erato, and Polyhymnia) were related to different forms of poetry (epic, romantic, ceremonial) and two to theater arts (Melpomene to tragedy and Thalia to comedy). Terpsichore was the muse of dance, and Euterpe the muse of music. The modern academic world has seven fine arts: painting, architecture, and sculpture are primarily visual arts; poetry and music are related to hearing; dance and theater are considered performance arts. And, of course, there are the storytellers, from troubadour to novelist to Garrison Keillor.

Art has always included the paired relationship of designing and making. Often these functions go together, as in the writer-director of a film, or a potter designing and creating ceramics. But they can be separate, as in the performer versus the playwright, the inventor versus the machinist, or the novelist versus the publisher.

At its root, art is anything that creates or recombines elements in an original way. It seeks to represent harmony and beauty while showing, in the elements chosen, a deep truth. Art teaches—but not didactically. Instead it shows and reveals what would not otherwise be seen or heard.

The artist path can be a consuming lifework; it can also be a little songwriting on the weekend. It isn't about quality or quantity; it's just the act of creating.

Combining Paths

Often, elements of the six life paths are blended. Many novelists go beyond storytelling; they seek to teach, to uncover truths about human relationship. Some warriors organize armies, or groups for social justice or competitive business. Some scientists both teach and heal; for example, professors who research new treatments for emotional problems and then use their discoveries to provide effective therapies. Some builders teach design and engineering. Some healers also fight for social change.

The ways in which paths combine are infinite. Many critical life tasks require skills from multiple paths. For example, parents *teach* their children, *heal* their pain and wounds, *explore* methods for solving family problems, and *guard* their children's safety. Few of us walk a single road. We have interests, talents, needs—and a life mission—that require integrating several pathways.

The following exercise will help you clarify which paths you've taken in this life and what you might want to change.

EXERCISE: Which Path Are You On?

This is an opportunity to learn which of the six paths you walk. For each of the following paths listed, write what **percentage** of your productive time is spent doing things related to that path. This includes things you do at home, at work, with friends and family, and with your community. You may find that you do things associated with several of the paths, so enter percentages for each. For example, one person who did this exercise spent 40 percent of her time on the teaching path, and 20 percent each as an activist (warrior) and artist. Notice that the total percentage of your time spent on all paths can add up to less than 100 percent. Depending on the level of commitment to your path, this total percentage could range from small to large. When you walk several paths, pay attention to the relative time spent on each. In the next part of the exercise, you'll have an opportunity to make new choices about this.

Percent of Productive Time	Life Path
	Teacher/Communicator
	Healer/Peacemaker
	Warrior/Guardian
	Explorer/Scientist
	Builder/Organizer
	Artist/Designer

Look over the percentages. These are the paths your soul has chosen for pursuing your life mission, your destiny. Now ask yourself this question: *Is this who I want to be?* While your paths were probably chosen by your soul before birth, how much time and commitment you give to each path could change substantially. Would you, if you could allot your energy and time differently, rebalance your commitments? If so, return to the chart and fill in these alternative percentages.

The path you are on, and the scale of your activities, doesn't matter. What matters is being on a path, a mission—and walking it with intention and purpose.

12

YOUR MISSION: FIVE WAYS TO FIND AND ALIGN WITH YOUR LIFE PURPOSE

As we have pointed out from the beginning of this book, each of us arrives on the planet with a predetermined purpose, a preconception contract, as it were. It will fit snugly into the purpose of the entire species, which is to lift our consciousness into a state of harmony with the evolutionary trajectory of life itself. It is of paramount importance that each of us discover this purpose and align fully with it. This chapter will offer several techniques for uncovering this life purpose.

It is easy to become complacent or to lose focus and forget. So it is very useful to periodically engage in some formal kind of self-exploration, perhaps on your birthday, at New Year's, or at the start of a new phase of life (such as starting school, college, a new job, or a marriage; or the birth of a child). It is good to mark these transitions by looking within. To do justice to it, you need to find a time and a place where you will be undisturbed for a couple of hours.

For major transitions it will be useful to do several of these exploration exercises in a short period of time (for example, over a weekend). For more regularly occurring seasons (such as the start of spring or summer), perhaps choose one exercise just to stir up some mindfulness.

Familiarize yourself with the following kinds of explorations, and when you decide to devote some time to a deeper exercise, listen for your gut response in order to choose among the exercises.

The Hero's Journey

When a young, wild elephant is being trained, it is tied to an experienced, working elephant for many weeks before it can be ridden by the trainer (the mahout).

Imitation is both the highest form of flattery and an efficient way to learn a new skill.

A similar system shows up in human development. Children learn by being yoked to a family and a culture, and by learning to imitate. They learn language and accent, but also values, prejudices, ideals, fears, hopes, confidence, and despair. They imitate dress code, walking style, and eating habits, and are cued to the use of alcohol, tobacco, drugs, and sexuality.

They organize their own lives around the powerful archetype of the hero and seek inspiration from both public personalities and private relationships. A lot of money and media promotion will offer a slew of sports stars, actors and actresses, supermodels and musicians as subjects worthy of admiration and imitation. Occasionally, a Mother Teresa will achieve superstar status. And the results are both social and psychological. In the book *Human Motivation*, Harvard researcher David McClelland reported his finding that just watching a movie of Mother Teresa's work leads to an immediate strengthening of the viewer's immune system.

But personal heroes can also come from your own family or circle of acquaintances, and can exert quite an influence, whether it leads to joining a gang or the Peace Corps.

Here are some of our heroes: A friend was paralyzed in a diving accident as a young man but went on to become a very accomplished attorney who has advocated nationally and internationally for the rights of the disabled. As a child in Dublin, Ireland, Christine Nobel lived on the streets and was sexually assaulted more than once. Yet prompted by a vivid dream about a young Vietnamese girl calling out to her for help, she went on to found several orphanages in Vietnam. Gandhi's expulsion from a first-class railway carriage in South Africa was the catalyst for a lifelong commitment to Ahimsa, peaceful rebellion against injustice and oppression.

Are these the kinds of heroes *you* might want to imitate? Perhaps there are different qualities that you want to develop. So think of people whom *you* hold as heroes and identify the qualities that appeal to you.

It's a truism that your character can be inferred from the company you keep—not just your social company, but also the intrapsychic company of your own thoughts. So, whose images align you with your core rather than merely arouse a self-serving agenda? Whom do you admire? Whose lives display the values that matter most to you?

EXERCISE: Your Heroes

This is a chance to look at how individuals (whether known personally to you or public figures) used a particular attribute to define or discover *their* life purpose. Explore the role of each hero in your life by answering the following questions and doing the following practice on a piece of paper.

1. Make a list of five such individuals.

2. Highlight the trait you most admire in each person.

3. Rate how well the person manifests that trait on a scale from 1 (very poorly developed) to 10 (perfectly developed).

4. Now rate yourself on that same scale for that attribute.

5. Decide on some action to bridge the gap between your score and your hero's score.

The River of Life

"The best way to *predict* the future is to *create* it," said Abraham Lincoln. And the most trusted way to create the future is to live the present moment fully, because the present moment (no matter how it may *feel* to you) is nothing more and nothing less than the logical, consistent, inevitable consequence of all the decisions made by all of the players in the past. There is nothing miraculous or unlucky about it. It is what the participants have crafted. And when we work consciously with the present moment, we give birth to a future that is the logical, consistent, inevitable consequence of all the decisions we and others make right now.

The future is not some fated outcome decided on by an uncaring divinity or foisted upon us by a deterministic set of cosmic laws. Rather, the future is merely probable; it depends on forces of nature to create the environmental context, but it is the choices and the decisions of the *human* players that lead to the social and cultural outcomes.

One way to understand the present moment is to trace its trajectory from your birth to this time. An enlightening and practical way to do that is to divide your life into seven-year segments, and for each segment, note these three aspects: the important players, the important events, and the important lessons learned (either then or retrospectively).

You are the living embodiment of your past, the great rope formed by these three major strands. In level plains, rivers meander, while in steep terrains, they tend to take the shortest route. When we live life mindlessly, we, too, meander aimlessly, sometimes even looping back on our own progress; when we live life with wisdom, it is a much shorter journey to the realization of our dreams and alignment with our missions.

EXERCISE: Your River of Life

Now let's begin the exploration. On a separate piece of paper, create a template with four columns: the first one for the blocks of years, for example, 0–7, 8–14, 15–21, and so on; the second column for the major players; the third one for the major events; and the fourth one for the major lessons.

Now ask yourself: *Am I happy with how my river is flowing? What changes do I want to make in my relationships, work, home, and so on to redirect the course and the speed of the journey?*

As an example, suppose you discover that you've been abandoned by major figures throughout your life: a parent, a friend, a spouse. Does this mean that life sucks, or is it an invitation to develop deep inner strength that facilitates self-reliance and empowerment, and may also be very attractive to others, leading to more-permanent, faithful relationships?

Developing a Personal Cosmology

Everybody already has a personal cosmology (philosophy of life), but for the vast bulk of us, it is totally unconscious. It has been unconsciously acquired from family, school, media, churches, and so on, and when faced with any life situation, it is unconsciously accessed in a series of knee-jerk responses that may or may not serve us well. The greatest—in fact, the only—"sin" in life is the decision to stay unconscious. Every conscious decision (whether it leads to worldly success or apparent failure) can assist our growth. But being unconscious is a *guarantee* of suffering. Life demands that we snap out of the cultural trance, because for the most part, it is predicated on a cultural cosmology that is hopelessly out of date. To remind you briefly, this outdated cosmology is that which tells you, "The secret to happiness is to avoid pain and seek pleasure." This antiquated paradigm is the equivalent of trying to use a fifteenth-century map of the "New World" to make your way from Houston to San Francisco.

Reasoning science can help in developing our cosmology. Basically, the scientific method operates in one of two ways: the inductive method and the deductive method.

Induction is the technique of examining specific data and inferring (inducing) a principle from it. For example, you begin to ponder the fact that several times in the last couple of months, you have suffered from insomnia, which, up to then, was very unusual for you. You wonder why, and then realize that each time, it was after a visit to your friend Mike's house, where he served you caffeinated tea after dinner. Suddenly a brand-new principle has emerged: drinking caffeinated tea after 6:00 p.m. leads to insomnia that night.

Or look at the great Mayan sky gazers of a thousand years ago. The Mayans noted a change in the orientation of the winter-solstice sun vis-à-vis the center of the Milky Way galaxy and, by keeping careful records over many years, inferred the 25,920-year precession of the equinoxes.

Deduction goes in the opposite direction. It begins with an accepted principle and then applies it to a new situation. For example, a famous syllogism started with the principle "All men are mortal" and then deduced that since Socrates is a man, he, too, must be mortal. Or to go back to an earlier example, *It's my night to have dinner at Mike's, and I remember the recently acquired principle "Drink caffeinated tea after 6:00 p.m., and toss and turn all night long," so I politely decline the beverage after our delightful meal.*

117

The science of personal growth, then, is the ability to balance induction (things you figure out for yourself) and deduction (applying your own personal insights or the insights of others to new situations).

Faced, then, with any life situation, you basically have three choices:

- Inductively infer a brand-new principle. This is the way of creativity and is hugely satisfying.

- Deductively apply an old principle from your *own* repertoire. This is the ability to recognize that the new situation has many features of a previous one and can benefit from older experiences and the lessons they taught.

- Borrow a pertinent principle from *another* source. This ensures that you are not wasting time trying to reinvent the wheel, but rather are pressing into service previously invented wheels.

Let us take a typical human situation and illustrate how you might use these three approaches. Suppose you are feeling down, putting on unwanted weight, and confused as to your direction in life.

An example of the first approach might be: *Nobody is going to solve this for me; I need to get creative and do this for myself.* A use of the second approach might add, *In the past, whenever I felt lethargic or depressed, I discovered that exercising outdoors helped a lot. So let me get my running shoes on.* And approach number three might say, *Native Americans would go on a vision quest to help them find direction during a significant time of life. Perhaps I might think of doing a vision quest myself.*

The beauty of using a previous principle (yours or another's) is that you can attach to an established wisdom network. The danger is that it may no longer be relevant; for example, *My country, right or wrong* or *Put your money in X; it's too big to fail.* The Buddha, though himself an accomplished teacher, went to great lengths to insist that each student be "a lamp unto yourself." And Socrates was executed for advocating that his students think for themselves and not just give blind obedience to the "truths" of the time.

Responding to life, then, is a dance between the inductive and deductive steps.

EXERCISE: Your Personal Cosmology

Here is an exercise on how to construct your personal cosmology. Let the players, events, and lessons of the previous exercise be the raw data for this exercise.

1. On one sheet of paper, write five principles that you are **freshly** inferring from these data.

2. On a second sheet of paper, write five principles that you have learned either from others or from your own **previous** insights that strike you as pertinent to these data.

These ten principles will be some of the key elements of your personal cosmology. Examine the inductive and deductive principles to determine which ones are liberating you and which ones are imprisoning you, because both inductive and deductive principles can sometimes be faulty.

For example, it might look like this for a person: "On the basis of reviewing my life in seven-year chunks, I freshly infer the following inductive principles: 'I need to ask for what I want, not expect people to guess,' 'Getting moody hurts me more than the people I'm upset with,' 'I'm happiest when I keep to a regular schedule,' 'Eating late at night leads to acid reflux,' and 'Family members are always there for me.'"

And this life review might throw up the following deductive principles, either from the wisdom of others or your own previous insights: "It's not life that hurts; it's the interpretations we foist on it that hurt." "My adversaries are every bit as convinced that they are right as I am convinced that I'm right." "Don't judge somebody until you've walked a mile in his moccasins." "Familiarity breeds contempt." "Don't sweat the small stuff."

Surveying the Self

False identity is when we think we are our bodies, our beliefs, or our emotional reactions, or even the professions we're in or the roles we play. False identity is when we mistake ethnicity, religious affiliation, or socioeconomic status for our real selves.

True identity, on the other hand, is when we glow from the inside, when the eternal, unborn part of us directs our thoughts, words, and deeds.

Imagine that you are trying to survey a countryside: if you stay down in the valley, your impressions of the terrain will be quite limited, but if you climb the highest hill in the area, then you get a panoramic vista. False identity is what keeps you stuck in the valley, whereas true identity is what makes you willing to climb the mountain. Your success as a cartographer is intimately correlated with the altitude of your viewpoint. Every increase in elevation allows you to shed a previous identity and adopt a new one. By the time you reach the mountaintop, your vision is far less limited.

The good news, however, is that there are probably even higher mountains to climb. If you want to be really, really happy, find them and scale them.

True Identity vs. False Identity

Here are some typical statements that help you recognize when you were in true identity: "I was contented then." "I was poor as a church mouse but happy as a clam." "I was in the flow, in the zone." "Things didn't get to me." "I looked forward to each new day." "I never woke in the morning with a sense of foreboding." "The last thing I used to do at night was to give a great sigh of satisfaction and then sleep like a baby." "I smiled a lot at people, and they smiled back." "I felt that I was making the world a better place." "I felt ageless and powerful."

Christ once said, "You must be compassionate as your heavenly father is compassionate." He was speaking in Aramaic, a language in which the word "compassion" (*rahamim*) is the plural of the word for "womb." So a better translation of the injunction would be, "You must be womblike, even as is the birthing principle of the universe." A womb is an organ that can conceive, carry, and birth life—many times, not just once. And that is how you develop from false identity to true identity: by sequentially disidentifying with lesser senses of self, and birthing and identifying with greater senses of self. You will encounter many *temporary* identities in the course of this journey. Identity is not a binary choice between false and true, but a position on a spectrum. Each new position will help you grow beyond the last identity, but others will continue to beckon until you've reached your true identity.

EXERCISE: "Will the Real Me Please Stand Up?"

Grab a sheet of paper and create two columns: (1) the seven-year chunks of your life and (2) your primary identity. Ask yourself, *What was my primary identity during that phase?* After examining each phase and each successive identity, ask, *What is my primary identity now?* Then ask, *Am I prepared to disidentify even with this one?* and *If so, what will be my* next *identity?*

Let's consider two examples: From 0–7 perhaps your identity was being "a good boy"; then from 8–14 you believed yourself to be "the rebel"; from 15–21 you saw yourself as "the great experimenter"; from 22–28 you saw yourself as "the sensible one"; from 29–35, you saw yourself as "the business-person";

from 36–42, you saw yourself as "the parent." Now, in this current phase, you see yourself as "the mentor," and perhaps during the next phase, you will see yourself as "the seeker after truth."

And a second example might be: From 0–7 perhaps your identity was being "Daddy's little princess"; then from 8–14 you believed yourself to be "the good student"; from 15–21 you saw yourself as "the pretty one"; from 22–28 you saw yourself as "a career academic"; from 29–35, you saw yourself as "the mother"; from 36–42 you saw yourself as "the community leader." Now, in this current phase, you see yourself as "the grandmother," and perhaps during the next phase, you will see yourself as "the wise one who shows the way."

So, as you revisit each era, by recalling the people and the events, and recognize the identity you adopted during that period, listen to your gut. Is it roiling with regret and contracting with contrition, or is it relaxed and rejoicing? Your heart will soon choose for you among the past identities and tell you, *Yes, that one really suited you; you were at your best*. Then identifying with your true self and recognizing your mission become easy. You're on the path.

EXERCISE: Reality Check

Now comes the time to "walk the talk," to begin living your life according to your personal cosmology. It's where the rubber meets the road. The exercise itself is based on a very simple self-inquiry that creates an orienting mechanism to navigate you through your daily choices. It goes like this: Pick out five important issues from your past and five important present-day issues. For example, you might pick issues such as follows:

1. A significant relationship that turned out well

2. A significant relationship that turned out badly

3. A health problem you encountered

4. A situation you had to deal with in your work life

5. A financial issue you had to contend with

Now ask yourself, *If I really believed that (a) I am an immortal soul (b) who volunteered for this particular life (c) in order to fulfill my unique mission, how would I respond to this event or person? How would awareness of my mission influence my behavior?* In other words, *If I believe I am a soul that signed up for an Earth mission, then how would I act in each of these circumstances?*

Now take a sheet of paper and list five past issues. Then see what might be the appropriate response based on the three beliefs (a, b, and c). Take a second sheet of paper and repeat the exercise for five *current* issues.

As an example, suppose you are diagnosed with a serious illness, and let's say that your normal modus operandi would be to freak out. Now, instead, you say to yourself, *I have a body,*

125

but I am not my body. I am an eternal being who will never die. This illness is only about the physical space suit. I will deal with the situation using common sense and availing myself of the reasonable options, but most important, I will remain steadfast in my mission. In the body or out of the body, my purpose is to love.

In this chapter we spoke of the preconception contract, which is to align with life's purpose of evolving into harmony with all of nature. And we gave you five practical techniques to help you do this: identifying and imitating your heroes, analyzing your life in seven-year chunks, developing a personal cosmology based on inductive and deductive principles, distinguishing between the false and the true self, and, finally, measuring all of your behavior against your remembered mission.

This is the equivalent of having a manual written personally for you, showing you how to operate your space suit. Use these exercises well and regularly, and your space suit will behave optimally. The mission will become obvious; your soul will soar, because it has been fully recognized, and your sense of satisfaction with life will be deep.

13

WHERE ARE
WE GOING?

We know that consciousness can exist outside the body and can move from body to body, lifetime to lifetime. We have evidence, from the research of Michael Newton and others, that our individual consciousness—the self—can exist in a "life between lives," where we learn and grow in a nonphysical environment. And we have reason to believe that we come to this planet to learn lessons that are only possible in a physical habitat, a place where every choice is made while we face a risk of pain or loss.

But what of consciousness as a whole? What relationship does the self, our individual conscious lives, have to the billions of other selves? What is the connection between your particular journey toward growth and wisdom, and the evolution of the whole, the collective sum of all conscious awareness in the universe? And, finally, what is the ultimate purpose of all this growing and evolving, of lesson learning in countless lifetimes by countless souls? Where does it go, and what is it used for?

A good place to start is looking at your *self*.

What Self Is

The self is a learning system designed to gather experience and knowledge. Just as bees have mandibles, wings, and legs for the sole purpose of gathering pollen, all the capabilities of self derive from our purpose: gathering and learning from experience. In order to learn, each self must be able to:

1. *Observe* experience.

2. *Remember* experience.

3. *Organize* experience (into categories and conclusions, or wisdom).

4. *Choose* actions (either mental actions, such as focusing attention, or behaviors, such as moving and communicating).

These four functions of self result in one thing: the ability to take what we've been through and turn it into practical knowledge. We are built to observe, remember, and evaluate the choices and events of our lives. This is the work of self, of soul, of consciousness.

Your Identity

Some people confuse identity and self. Identity is to self as a cover is to a book. It is the face of self. We learn to recognize ourselves by our cover, by familiar patterns of thinking, feeling, and behaving. Identity is built on a sentence that starts, "I am a person who…"

Identity includes emotions by which we know ourselves—for example, "I am a person who is… (angry, afraid, lonely)"—and the characteristic ways in which we cope; for example, "I am a person who… (cares, avoids, gives up, gets tough)." Identity born of reacting to life is left behind when we leave the body.

Identity that grows from what we've learned becomes part of self, of soul. It is an enduring core wisdom that evolves with each life. "I am a person who has realized…" is the place where self and identity merge, and is the reason why we are here.

The Self as Part of the Larger Whole

Each self, each soul, is a component of the whole of all consciousness. What each self learns becomes part of the collective awareness of all selves. So, for example, if you have struggled in a difficult relationship, and yet have learned to be loving in the face of that pain, the lessons learned become part of shared human wisdom. What we each discover is potentially held by all of us forever.

There is a universal memory (sometimes called the akashic record) that is like a doting grandparent who records everything each of the grandchildren does. Nothing is lost. All thoughts and deeds become grist for the mill of evolution.

Consider again the metaphor of the bee. A bee—the self, the soul, the individual consciousness—flies out from the hive to collect pollen. And so it is that we, in each life, come here to collect experiences, increase knowledge, and grow in wisdom. And then we bring back what we've learned to the collective consciousness. In each life we journey out from the hive—our life between lives—on a mission to grow, and then return with every experience we've gathered.

Our relationship to every other self, every other soul, is that of colearner, or fellow learner. And our relationship to the greater whole of evolving selves is that of a precious and eternal part. Each self is a unique source of knowledge and wisdom that contributes to the evolution of the whole. Just as each citizen contributes to a community and each wave rolls to make the endless movements of the sea, each self brings something to the whole of all selves, all consciousness. And the whole would be diminished without it.

Where To?

Every time you grow as a person, a self, all of humanity and all of life grows. But to what end? What is the point of evolving—as a self or collectively? The great scientist and philosopher Pierre Teilhard de Chardin talked about the stages of evolution and where they lead. It starts with the physiosphere (the rock called Earth) and develops into the hydrosphere (the oceans, lakes, and rivers) and the biosphere (all forms of life on the planet). Finally, with the development of consciousness that can reflect on itself, the noosphere evolves: a sheath of consciousness connecting all intelligence on the planet. The noosphere, if seen in computer terms, is like the cloud, where it is possible to both upload and download ideas. It's a place where you can post tweets and read blogs, a place where experience is collected and shared. And the noosphere itself evolves as more and more is posted on it.

Teilhard de Chardin spoke of the Omega Point, where we—our individual souls linked to all our collective wisdom—become godlike. This is not the personal god of world religions, but the divine self embodied in all collective knowledge, seeing and knowing, and with the power to create as yet undreamed of universes. The potentials of this divine being lie too far ahead to be understood or imagined. But we are heading there— together. And each step we take on our mission to learn is bringing us closer.

Some modern astronomers have postulated that our universe is simply a daughter universe of a metaverse, which is reborn continually and applies the learnings of past versions to its newest effort. And *who* is doing this learning? We are.

Atman and Jiva

It's easy to make posts or get information from the cloud. But the methods of communication with the noosphere—our collective consciousness—are more complex. A metaphor from Hindu theology may offer a key. The soul, according to Hindu beliefs, has two aspects. The one that undertakes incarnation on a regular basis is called *jiva*. The other part, *atman*, stays with the whole, the hive. It is the link to the collective consciousness and acts as an observer and guide to jiva. Meanwhile jiva, caught in a particular life, forgets almost everything about where we come from. But atman remembers our mission—why we came here—and stays in communication with jiva, gently reminding us of our purpose.

We stay in contact with atman through intuitive flashes, sudden insights, dreams, visions, déjà vu, synchronicities, inspiring teachers—even through illness and accidents. We can initiate this dialogue—with the noosphere, with collective consciousness, with god—in many ways: prayer, reflection, meditation, intuition, natural beauty, and just plain listening. This is all about getting quiet so that we can download—letting the noosphere talk.

Many traditional religious practices provide a conduit to the noosphere. They teach us to listen to a truth and wisdom that transcends our own personal knowledge.

Pain itself is an invitation to listen. As we struggle with losses, we inevitably ask, Why? And that question opens a channel to atman, to the collective knowledge that all of us share outside this physical life. If we listen, the question Why? begins the download, the intuitive sense of our mission. The specific answers may be different for everyone, but at the deepest level, our pain is the source of all learning.

Alignment

The collective consciousness, the whole, has a mission for the planet—changes that must be made to promote the growth of all souls. Our individual missions need to be brought into alignment with that of the whole—the health and well-being of all humanity, all life on Earth. So every choice we make needs to fit with the needs of souls around us and the larger community of those who populate the Earth. Each species to date has done so, finding its unique niche based on its own gifts and its own purpose. For example, underground fungi offer nitrogen to great trees in exchange for sun-sourced chlorophyll. Little fish clean the great teeth of killer sharks in exchange for leftovers.

Each self, each human soul, lives in relationship to all others, human and nonhuman. No choice exists in a vacuum, because via the ripple effect, it will eventually touch everyone else, bringing them closer to or farther away from their mission. So, for example, if a number of souls have for their mission the achievement of ecological balance or protecting particular groups that are oppressed, our choices need to be aligned with that. Doing things that damage what others are trying to protect occurs when we lose sight of our interrelatedness.

The Meaning of Forever

Learning and growth go on forever—for our "selves" and for the whole. Consciousness continues to expand. And as it does, it will create new—more elegant, more beautifully crafted—universes with which to interact and further evolve. Each choice we make, each lesson we learn moves us—and all consciousness—along this transcendent path.

Matthew McKay, PhD, is a professor at the Wright Institute in Berkeley, CA. He has authored and coauthored numerous books, including *The Relaxation and Stress Reduction Workbook*, *Self-Esteem*, *Thoughts and Feelings*, *When Anger Hurts*, and *ACT on Life Not on Anger*. He has also penned two fiction novels, *Us* and *The Wawona Hotel*. McKay received his PhD in clinical psychology from the California School of Professional Psychology, and specializes in the cognitive behavioral treatment of anxiety and depression. He lives and works in the Bay Area.

Seán ÓLaoire, PhD, is a Catholic priest and licensed clinical psychologist specializing in transpersonal psychology. ÓLaoire regularly lectures and conducts scientific research on the effects of prayer. In addition, he is cofounder and spiritual director of Companions on the Journey (COJ), a popular Silicon Valley spiritual community which seeks to recognize the God/divinity within the self. He has a private counseling practice in Los Altos, CA.

Ralph Metzner, PhD, is a licensed clinical psychologist and professor emeritus at the California Institute of Integral Studies in San Francisco, CA. He has authored and coauthored several books, including *The Unfolding Self*, *The Well of Remembrance*, *Green Psychology*, *The Roots of War and Domination*, *Know Your Type*, and *Sacred Vine of Spirits*.

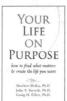

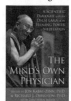